More Christmas Moments

More Christmas Moments

55 Stories of the True Meaning of Christmas

COMPILED AND EDITED BY YVONNE LEHMAN

Scripture quotations marked NIV are taken from the *The Holy Bible, New International Version*. Copyright © 1973, 1978, 1984, International Bible Society. Used by permission of Zondervan. All rights reserved.

Scripture quotations marked NKJV taken from the New King James Version®. Copyright © 1982 by Thomas Nelson. Used by permission. All rights reserved.

Scripture quotations marked NLT are taken from the *Holy Bible, New Living Translation*, copyright © 1996. Used by permission of Tyndale House Publishers, Inc., Wheaton, Illinois 60189. All rights reserved.

Scripture quotations marked cev are taken from the *Contemporary English Version*, copyright © 1995 by American Bible Society. Used by permission. All rights reserved.

MORE CHRISTMAS MOMENTS
55 Stories of the True Meaning of Christmas

ISBN-13: 978-1-60495-017-5

Copyright © 2015 by Yvonne Lehman. Published in the USA by Grace Publishing. All rights reserved. No part of this book may be reproduced in any form or by any electronic or mechanical means, including information storage and retrieval systems, without permission in writing, except as provided by USA Copyright law.

From Samaritan's Purse

We so appreciate you donating royalties from the sale of the books *Divine Moments, Christmas Moments, Spoken Moments* and *Precious, Precocious Moments* and *More Christmas Moments* to Samaritan's Purse. What a blessing that you would think of us! Thank you for your willingness to bless others and bring glory to God through your literary talents. Grace and peace to you.

Their mission statement:

Samaritan's Purse is a nondenominational evangelical Christian organization providing spiritual and physical aid to hurting people around the world.

Since 1970, Samaritan's Purse has helped victims of war, poverty, natural disasters, disease, and famine with the purpose of sharing God's love through his son, Jesus Christ.

Go and do likewise. (Luke 10:37d)

You can find out more by visiting their website at www.samaritanspurse.org.

Dedication

Dedicated to
Terri Kalfas, who saw the beauty
and value of sharing praise
in
Divine Moments
Christmas Moments
Spoken Moments
Precious, Precocious Moments
and now makes it possible
for the sharing of
More Christmas Moments

and
to the writers who were so eager to share

and
to the readers we hope and pray will be blessed
by our stories as they were with our
other *Moments* collections

Contents

Introduction 9

1. Little Foxes *Yvonne Lehman* 11
2. The Christmas Truce *Dan Balow* 14
3. Trashing the Christ Child *Sandra Fischer* 16
4. How Santa Helps Me Remember the True Meaning of Christmas
   Diana Leagh Matthews 18
5. A Fresh New Christmas *Elsie H. Brunk* 20
6. At Birth and Silent Night of the Soul *Charlotte Adelsperger* 22
7. Two Christmases *Linda Landreth Phelps (as told to her by Fran Rahn)* ... 23
8. A Husband's Devotion *Rebecca Carpenter* 26
9. I Heard Him on the Roof *Carole A. Bell* 28
10. Mustard Seeds and Cheap Perfume *Bernadean J. Gates* 30
11. Christmas Legacy *Debbie Presnell* 33
12. Unexpected Guests for Christmas *Geneva Cobb Iijima* 35
13. An M&M Christmas *Theresa Jenner Garrido* 39
14. The Sparkling Bow of Joy *Janet Perez Eckles* 41
15. When the Most Wonderful Time of the Year Isn't *Julie Arduini* ... 45
16. The Light *Larry C. Hoover* 47
17. Picture Perfect Christmas *Barbara Latta* 49
18. The Question *Nate Stevens* 51
19. A Flash of Red *Dee Dee Parker* 53
20. Plug-ins *Carlitta Cole-Kelly* 55
21. Christmas Presence *Annmarie B. Tait* 58
22. The Story *Sondra Kraak* 61
23. Christmas Potpourri *Joann Claypoole* 63
24. An Unexpected Christmas Gift *Joyce Heiser* 65
25. Gwen's Silent Night *Susan Holt Simpson* 68
26. The Christmas Tree Brooch *Joni Vance* 71

27. What a Gift! *Diana Derringer* 73
28. Christmas Came *Charlotte Adelsperger* 75
29. Counting Southern Treasures Through the First Noel *Vicki H. Moss* 76
30. A Pure and Simple King *Ann Tatlock* 81
31. Plan a Silent Night *Lydia E. Harris* 83
32. Provision in a Time of Need *Marybeth Mitcham* 85
33. Sunshine for Christmas *Lisa Braxton* 89
34. Christmas Caper *Karen R. Hessen* 92
35. When God Heals a Christmas Memory *Cathy Baker* 95
36. Jesus in a Barn *Kimberly Rae* 97
37. Favored by His Death *Cindy Sproles* 99
38. Steeped in Christmas Tradition *Victoria Hicks* 101
39. Make Peace with the Past *Sheryl Baker* 104
40. How Could I Manage Without It? *Carol Graham* 106
41. The Warmth of Christmas *Autumn J. Conley* 108
42. The Last Doll *Dianne Neal Matthews* 110
43. The Birth That Saves *Emme Gannon* 113
44. Finding Baby Jesus *Marybeth Mitcham* 115
45. Are You There, Lord? *Ann Greenleaf Wirtz* 118
46. Ghost of Christmas Past *Simon Wilson* 121
47. Presence for Christmas *Edie Melson* 124
48. Come Dance with Me *Dr. Rhett Wilson* 126
49. Am I Good Enough? *Andrea Merrell* 128
50. Suzy Snowflake and the Blue Christmas Turned White *Vicki H. Moss* 130
51. From My Heart to Theirs *Esther M. Bailey* 134
52. You Are Christmas *Joann Claypoole* 136
53. Christmas Retreat *Sheryl M. Baker* 138
54. Poor Baby Jesus *Susan Dollyhigh* 140
55. Setting Goals *Yvonne Lehman* 142
About the Authors 144

Introduction

"Bah, humbug!"

Ebenezer Scrooge spoke those words in Charles Dickens' novella, *A Christmas Carol,* in response to his nephew saying, "Merry Christmas!" The words Scrooge used to express his disgust with Christmas traditions are often used today by some who don't care for contemporary Christmas traditions.

So memorable is Scrooge's attitude, even his name now symbolizes those who are miserly, have disdain for others, or care only about themselves.

The story is one of redemption, however, as the three Ghosts of Christmas (Ghost of Christmas Past, Ghost of Christmas Present, and Ghost of Christmas Yet to Come) take Scrooge on a journey.

Due to the messages of the visiting ghosts, Scrooge begins to experience a change in personality. He has a second chance. The story shows that even the hardest heart can be softened. Scrooge changes into a man who cares about others. At the end of the story it is said of him, "His own heart laughed…and it was always said of him, that he knew how to keep Christmas well."

A Christmas Carol is a fictional redemption story. As Christians, we know that change in our lives is brought about by the Holy Ghost (or Holy Spirit) when we accept Jesus as our Savior and journey with him in our lives.

Many of the stories in this book depict change. Some are about the difficulty of facing Christmas, the sadness of loss and grief, the hurt of some Christmas memories, but even in those the authors come to a realization of the true meaning of Christmas and the reason to celebrate or "keep Christmas well."

Other stories are happy childhood memories, the joy of the season, the beauty and excitement of the holiday.

Here are a few comments about our first *Christmas Moments* book:

"I just finished reading *Christmas Moments* this morning. It is fantastic and I am proud to be part of it. Hope we can do another Christmas one sometime. I particularly enjoyed 'going with you' on your trip to the Holy Land. I felt as if I had stowed away in your luggage and was right there." ~ Colleen Reece

"My editor at *American Daily Herald* ordered *Christmas Moments* after advertising the book on the newspaper's website for me. Thought you would like to read her feedback:

> I have set aside a small amount of time right before bed to read *Christmas Moments*. I have been reading only a few stories a night so I can enjoy it throughout the season. But it has been so hard to put the book down. The stories have made me laugh and cry and have given me a few odd looks from Dennis [her husband]….articles give me so much happiness (goosebumps & tears included) to read! I am about halfway through the book and don't want it to end. What a wonderful blessing this book is!

"I've sent a copy of the book to a woman I mentor in prison — can't wait to get feedback from her as well." ~ Vicki Moss

In February 2015, Diana Flegal (agent and *Moments* book contributor) and I (Yvonne) were on a plane to a writers conference in Florida. We talked briefly with the man in the window seat who was going to Florida on business. He asked where we were going, and in talking about writing, I gave him a copy of *Christmas Moments*. He was impressed that the authors donated their stories and that royalties would go to Samaritan's Purse. He knew of Billy Graham but asked questions about Samaritan's Purse. Our conversation with him ended. When we were about to land, he leaned forward to say he had read the first and another article. He hesitated, then told us about going to a Billy Graham crusade many years ago. His wife was curious and wanted to go down when the invitation was given. He didn't want to but went with her. "It meant a lot to her," he said. Then he gave me a generous donation for Samaritan's Purse.

You just never know what these articles will mean to others…but God knows!

As Tiny Tim says in *A Christmas Carol*, "God bless Us, Every One!"

~ *Yvonne Lehman*

❧ 1 ❦
Little Foxes

It was two days before Christmas. I'd spent most of the morning preparing to teach the Sunday school class on Sunday. One of the things I read and planned to share was that saying "Merry Christmas" implies "Jesus' Birthday." Saying "Merry Christmas" can mean to other Christians what drawing a fish in the dirt meant to early Christians. It means I'm a believer, I'm a follower.

I felt good about the lesson. Getting the Christmas spirit, I went to the drug store to buy a small tree that would be a Promise Tree. A person on an email loop had mentioned her family does that each Christmas. She prints out God's promises and fastens them on a tree. Others pick one off. The following year each person tells how the promise they picked was fulfilled in their life during the past year.

I wanted to do that. I had also planned a Giving Box, in which my grandchildren would decide upon and donate money to a charity or a needy family. That would teach them not to just receive, but to give.

So, having planned spiritual ways to celebrate the true meaning of Christmas, I felt good — like a good Christian should.

Then I drove to the post office, which closes at noon on Saturday. I saw the postmaster outside helping a young couple at their car. They must have locked the keys inside because the door on the driver's side was wedged open by a block of wood and the woman was pushing a stick down along the window on the inside.

I went in and retrieved my mail, which included a yellow card indicating I had a package or envelope too large for the box. Just then the postmaster and the man who had been at the car came inside. The postmaster unlocked the side door. I went over quickly, held out the yellow card and said, with a smile, "Could you get this for me?"

"I'm sorry, we're closed," he said.

I felt my eyes widen, along with my mouth. I gaped. I probably sneered.

"You can't get it for me?"

"No, we're closed," he repeated.

I inhaled audibly. "Merry Christmas!" I said.

He said something like, "You have a good one, too." He closed the door.

I was shocked and stood there a moment, stunned. Many times I've knocked on that door after closing time, and if anyone's there, they always get the package for me. No one had ever refused. They'd even done it with a smile.

I returned to my box, unlocked it, stuck the yellow card back in, slammed the little door, and locked it.

My blood was simmering as I drove up the street toward home.

Then it hit me!

What had I said to that man? The thought in my mind and the intent of my heart was not "Jesus is born."

No, it was more like saying, "I love you, too," when you really mean, "I don't like you."

I hadn't really meant "Merry Christmas." What I had intended to relay was that he was not exemplifying the Christmas spirit…because he didn't cater to me!

Then it occurred to me that having the Christmas spirit doesn't mean that one should do what I want. Having the Christmas spirit means honoring God and helping others. The postmaster apparently was helping that young couple. He was also keeping the rules about customers getting their mail during post office hours.

The previous week, the Sunday school lesson I had taught had been about the Ten Commandments — keeping God's laws and man's laws. Now I was chagrined because the postmaster had kept the post office rule. No, it wouldn't have hurt him to get my mail. But he was in no way obligated. He'd followed his employer's rules.

Tears came to my eyes as I realized what I'd done.

I thought about what Solomon wrote in Song of Songs 2:15: *Quick! Catch all the little foxes before they ruin the vineyard of your love, for the grapevines are all in blossom.*

Self-centered little foxes can mess up one's influence.

I've often thought that postal clerks know a lot about a person just by the mail they get. I receive a lot of mail. The clerks know me. They know my box number without even looking at what's written on those yellow cards. Most of my mail is about the Christian writers conference I plan, and from churches, Christian bookstores, and Christian publishers.

And yet, my saying "Merry Christmas" with a sneer could very well ruin whatever good influence my mail from Christian organizations could have built up. It only takes one sin or mistake to ruin a reputation.

I learned from that. How quickly, how easily, how sly are those little foxes so near the surface, ready to eat up what has been planted, tear up the vines.

I prayed then for God to forgive me and to cause the postmaster to believe that I really meant Merry Christmas. I prayed he would truly have a Merry Christmas.

~ *Yvonne Lehman*

2

The Christmas Truce

This is a tough world to figure out. Depending on your worldview, people are either inherently good with the bad habit of doing bad things, or they are inherently evil people who once in a while do something good and wonderful. Because of the belief in original sin, Christians generally adhere to the latter view.

Over one hundred years ago, on December 23, 1914, something wonderful happened, but it was quickly swallowed up by evil. The wonder remains to this day as a glimpse into what God intended humans to be. It was a microcosm of our world involving the same kind of conflicted people that consume our Christian messages and books.

The glimpse into hope occurred during the First World War. During a lull which occurred fighting in a major action near Ypres, Belgium, soldiers reported hearing hymns being sung from trenches on both sides. German soldiers were said to have brought Christmas trees to the Allied side in a gesture of peace.

The next day, on Christmas Eve, German snipers shot ninety-eight British soldiers, and a German aircraft dropped a bomb on Dover, England, the first air-raid in British history. So much for peace.

Yet, as the day wore on, British troops saw Christmas trees with candles pop up on the German lines. Carols, hymns and other songs were sung. Much of the communication between the two sides was to arrange for retrieving the bodies of dead comrades.

On Christmas day, 1914, units on both sides attended church services, ate Christmas dinners and over half of the front lines experienced a spontaneous truce at dozens of distinct points in France, Belgium and from the North Sea to the Swiss border. Some reported that soldiers on opposite sides exchanged addresses and they buried their dead in joint burial services.

But the truce was not honored everywhere. Some snipers would kill an enemy who came into their sights.

As the war plodded on, no "Christmas Truce" happened in 1915, 1916 or 1917. But for a brief moment over one hundred years ago, there was a glimmer of something new.

This doesn't seem like much of a Merry Christmas message, but I think it perfectly portrays the world into which we bring our message of hope.

It is a messy world. There are wonderful pockets of peace and terrible areas of evil. The points where they touch can be jarring.

But the hope remains, starting from a manger in Bethlehem and ending with God's promise that one day the baby will return as a conquering king and revert the world to the state in which it was originally created.

Keeping that hope in mind reminds us why we can have a Merry Christmas.

– Dan Balow

❦ 3 ❦
Trashing the Christ Child

Colored paper, empty boxes, tissue and ribbon covered our living room carpet, evidence that our family had once again lived up to the cultural expectations of Christmas gift-giving. We had engaged in the Christmas shopping frenzy to buy the gifts, spent Christmas Day in a rush to open them, and were engaged in what quickly followed — the clamor to clear the debris, dismantle the tree, pack away the decorations and get on to the next thing — a family ski trip the following day.

Our three daughters were busy with assigned tasks to hurry the cleanup along, when our oldest daughter lamented, "Jesus is missing."

"What do you mean, he's missing?"

"He's not here with Mary and Joseph."

"You're kidding, right?"

Our youngest chimed in, "Mom, you don't joke about losing the baby Jesus."

So the search began — everyone looking for the small gilded paper mâché figure of baby Jesus.

Storage boxes were re-opened and examined and furniture moved and checked under to no avail — baby Jesus was lost.

"Maybe we put him in the trash by accident," our middle daughter mused.

"How could we possibly have trashed the Christ child?"

"We've checked everywhere else."

While someone shook the bag of wadded papers, the swaddled figurine dropped to the floor and a unified shout of "Hooray!" went up.

Our oldest daughter wrapped the small figure in tissue and her younger sister patted the form as it was tucked away, "Now he's safe and put away until next year."

Safe? Put away until next year?

The words tore at the fabric of my heart, revealing a truth that had been covered by years of layering — a paper mâché celebration of Christmas that had obscured Christ himself.

Later after everyone was in bed, I stood at the window looking out on new-fallen snow and the Christmas lights God put in the sky. I was overtaken by a sense of shame and remorse. How easy to celebrate Christmas but miss it at the same time. How easy to get caught up in the trappings of Christmas — the food, the decorations, the glitter, our presents to each other — all of them good, but not what was best.

In the process our family had misplaced the main thing, the greatest gift. And then, even if we gave a cursory notice to the Christ child, we packed him away into the Christmas Closet of our lives, ready only to bring him out as a decoration for our party the next year.

The melting snow trickling down the window matched the tears streaming down my face. I choked a prayer. *Lord, forgive us for making ourselves the center of attention and forgetting whose birthday it is. Thank you for showing me that without the gift of your Son I would be lost. May he have the prominence in my heart he deserves for each day of the year and particularly so at Christmas. Help me to redeem the Christ of Christmas and keep him foremost in celebrating its meaning.*

Not only did we find the baby Jesus we thought we had lost that year, we found a new regard toward celebrating Christmas. We still give gifts, but we are more deliberate about what we choose and we give special attention to keeping Christ where he is supposed to be — at the center of our celebration.

I will always treasure the lesson I learned that Christmas — God's gentle reminder of whose birthday it is and why he is the most precious present of all.

~ Sandra Fischer

4

How Santa Helps Me Remember the True Meaning of Christmas

While walking through the Christmas Shoppe in Gatlinburg, Tennessee, I stopped in my tracks.

Hanging on the wall was an ornament of the Christ child lying in the manger. Next to the manger Santa, with a baby lamb beside him, kneeled with his hands clasped and head bowed, as he gazed adoringly at our newborn Lord and Savior.

That was the first time I had seen this ornament, and it took mind back to a very special Christmas tradition I have.

Each year I attend The Singing Christmas Tree at a local church. I look forward to the event and begin checking for the dates of the performance and availability of tickets by October of each year. The performance is a wonderful time of worship, as the story of Christ's birth is told through song and drama.

However, the most touching part of the performance comes at the end of the cantata. The church usually sings "Wise Men Still Seek Him" or "O Come All Ye Faithful" to express the meaning and importance of this moment. The drama begins with the three Wise Men and their entourage, dressed in full regalia, approaching the Christ child and presenting their gifts of gold, frankincense and myrrh.

However, the presentation is far from being finished as the song continues. This is where I always grow teary eyed as people of today, such as a nurse, businessman, soldier, fireman, policeman, and school-age child approach the Christ child and kneel or salute to our Lord.

Most importantly, it is the last person that approaches our Lord that always chokes me up. It is a great reminder that while we have wonderful traditions, we need to keep the true meaning of Christmas in our hearts and minds.

As Santa approaches the baby Jesus, kneels and bows his head in acknowledgement that this infant child is the true reason we celebrate the season, I am reminded that all of the secular parts of Christmas will one day pass away. But the Christ child will never leave nor forsake me. Without fail, tears fill my eyes at this scene.

As the song comes to a close, one of the wise men approaches the baby Jesus and takes him from his mother, Mary. After cradling the infant for a moment, he holds the child high in the air in praise to God as the room inevitably fills with applause for the Christ.

I am brought back to the present, standing in the Christmas Shoppe, as I take an ornament from the wall. I know without a doubt I have to have this ornament.

A decade has passed since that time and the ornament or a figurine of this scene can easily be found today in a variety of places. I have grown my collection from that first precious ornament, but I still love the sweet reminder the scene provides.

I love having the reminder around the house that amid all of the hustle and bustle of the Christmas season, even Santa stops to remember the true reason for the season. That reason is the birth of our Lord and Savior, Jesus Christ.

~ Diana Leagh Matthews

5

A Fresh New Christmas

"God, please let me experience Christmas in a fresh, new way this year," I prayed.

It was early December and I was looking forward to my usual Christmas baking and decorating so I could entertain family and friends. My husband, Harry, had gone out of town for a week to help our son build in a new kitchen. That meant I had to do some of his daily tasks, like carrying in wood. It was a hard job and time-consuming, since it took me six to eight trips to the woodpile to fill our woodbox inside. I had to keep at it though, because the wood stove was our only source of heat.

In addition to the extra duties, it became necessary for me to stay with our two young grandsons every afternoon after school. Also, a close friend was going through a depression and needed encouragement and a listening ear.

"Oh well. When Harry gets home, I'll still have time to prepare for Christmas," I reasoned.

However, at the end of the week, Harry called. "This job is taking longer than we thought it would. I'm not sure when I'll be home."

Our youngest daughter called. "We won't be able to come for Christmas. I'm so sorry, Mom." This would be her first Christmas away from home.

Then the rest of our family decided we wouldn't get together until January. *Some Christmas this is going to be!* I inwardly lamented.

When I had prayed to experience Christmas in a fresh new way, I had expected to feel a special joy and excitement. Now it seemed that everything possible was happening to make me feel the opposite. Finally, one day I questioned God. "Didn't you hear my prayer? If so, why am I feeling so sad?"

As if in answer, thoughts about the very first Christmas came to my mind. Did Jesus feel sad when he had to leave his Father and beautiful heavenly home to become human on earth? How did it make Jesus feel to know that many people would reject his ministry?

I thought about Mary and Joseph. No doubt their plans were changed when they had to make the trip to Bethlehem. And so late in Mary's pregnancy. They wouldn't have the support of family and friends in Nazareth at this important time in their lives. Was Mary disappointed and sad when she had to give birth to her first baby in a lowly animal stable? Surely her mother-heart desired something better for her baby.

Then I thought again of my own situation. I could identify with Mary's feelings of disappointment and sadness because her plans had been changed. Mine had too.

Harry came home three days before Christmas. I still had not done any decorating or baking. Our Christmas day was quiet, with just the two of us. I had time to think about the real meaning of the day and how God's plan for Mary was better than any human plan would have been. In the quietness of the stable, Mary could reflect on the birth of Jesus and the events surrounding it. It was the perfect setting for her to experience the peace and wonder of it all.

I reflected too, on the events of the past few weeks in my own life and realized that God's plan for me was better than mine. He had been answering my prayer all along. I was experiencing Christmas in a fresh new way. I felt wonder and a deep peace.

I learned some new things about Christmas that year. Sadness can have a place in this special season. Perhaps it causes us to experience more deeply the joy and wonder of Jesus' birth. I learned too, that ministering to my family and friends, as I had done before Christmas, is more important than baking and decorating. Didn't Jesus come to minister to others? *The Son of man did not come to be served, but to serve, and to give his life as a ransom for many.* (Matthew 20:28 NIV)

But the most important thing I learned is that in order to have a meaningful Christmas, it isn't necessary to do all the usual things in preparation, or to have the kind of celebration we've always had. All we have to do is open our hearts to the wonder of Jesus' birth.

~ Elsie H. Brunk

6

At Birth

Jesus, Son of God, was
born of a young woman;
cradled in her loving arms —
held close to her heart.

Spiritually I am a child of God,
given newness through Christ;
cradled in everlasting arms —
held always to His heart.

~ Charlotte Adelsperger

Silent Night of the Soul

It can come…
a silent night of the soul
any time, any place —
Christ's presence,
personalized for your needs,
emanating heavenly peace.

~ Charlotte Adelsperger

❦ 7 ❦

Two Christmases

For the first twenty-five years of our marriage we would drive for hours to celebrate with our distant families. "It's logical, Fran," my husband, Rick Rahn, would tell me. "We have no children to pack up, no trunk full of Santa gifts."

That was seven years ago, before we became parents in our mid-fifties, before our world changed forever.

Our church, Williamsburg Community Chapel, sponsored a choir of forty orphans who came to Virginia in 2008 for a Christmas concert series. I hosted the adults who accompanied them, which led to my involvement in the Heart for Orphans ministry begun by a fellow Chapel member, Nancy Hathaway. The ministry supports Ukrainian orphanages and adoptions, both international and domestic. Since I had once worked at a small group home for teenaged children when we lived in upstate New York, I went to Berdyansk, Ukraine with Nancy to help set up a similar program.

While there, something unexpected happened. I called my husband in Williamsburg and told him, "I've fallen in love!"

There was a silent pause on his end, then I heard Rick give a big whoosh of relief as I went on. "There's a girl who's captured my heart, and we either have to adopt her or move to Ukraine to be with her."

"Can we talk about this when you get back, Fran?" Rick asked.

"Sure, just as long as you say yes."

As it turned out, this girl later chose to stay in Ukraine, but she was the catalyst for our expanded family.

One of the children in the visiting choir, Yana, had been tentatively matched with an American family for future adoption. During my mission trip to the orphanage I snapped Yana's picture, then put it on the refrigerator when I returned to the States, to remind us to pray for her. Each time Rick passed by, he would touch her photo and say, "This girl's heart jumps out at me."

Yana's adoption stalled as she was about to turn fifteen, just one short year away from the birthday that marks aging-out of the system, when the state releases orphans to make their own way in life.

Rick and I felt God had orchestrated it all and that Yana was meant be our daughter. He and I spent seven weeks in Ukraine during the holidays as part of the adoption process, so we were able to experience a typical Christmas in the orphanage.

The children decorated a tree, acted out skits, and on the 25th received a colorful Samaritan's Purse shoebox stuffed with school supplies, gloves, and hats. The Orthodox Christmas Day was spent in prayer and feasting. Following Ukrainian custom, we exchanged gifts on New Year's Day and enjoyed fireworks with Yana.

Yana was fortunate and unusual for an orphan because she had a cousin who had always made sure she had a personal gift to unwrap. Almost all possessions are communal in an orphanage. When clothing has to be laundered, unless a child washes the item by hand, there's no guarantee they'll get the same garment again.

After five years as an orphan, Yana came home with us. A few weeks later, we got word that her brother, Kolya, who was then twelve, had been placed in the orphanage. We began praying and asking God what we should do. Within a matter of months we were able to reunite Kolya with his sister after seven years of separation.

But God wasn't finished yet.

While we had been in Berdyansk to adopt Yana, a quiet little girl named Rita broke free of her shyness to laugh and give Rick a hug. That hug left a permanent impression on his heart and on mine. We kept her photo displayed and prayed for her regularly.

"If I were ever to go back to Ukraine to adopt again, I'd go for Rita," Rick would say.

Just before she turned sixteen and became ineligible for adoption, Rita joined our family in Virginia.

Family holidays are very different now. Before we became parents, gifts to each other weren't elaborate and our emphasis was always outward. Our greatest joy was giving, and it still is. We are now committed to honor the

Ukrainian heritage of our three children by celebrating Jesus' birth in our own home. First comes an old-fashioned, traditional American Christmas, followed by another celebration on January 7th, which happens to be both my birthday and Orthodox Christmas Day.

Waking up on Christmas morning to evidence that Santa had come was at first a difficult transition for the children, almost overwhelming. As parents, it was hard for Rick and me not to overbuy, because they needed everything from underwear to toys.

Kolya came to us with one small plastic bag clutched in his hand. Rita spent her first Christmas with us holding onto a single gift, reluctant to move on to another. Her next holiday was much easier, and by then she had made a total mental switch to American-style Christmas. Kolya definitely has the Bible story of Jesus' birth in his heart.

Rick and I didn't decorate much in the past. It wasn't important then, but now the children are establishing Christmas traditions of their own. I wanted to get a real tree for them, but they enjoy fitting the branches of an artificial one into the sockets. On Christmas morning we eat breakfast slowly, then talk and laugh as each one unwraps a gift. I like to include others at our holiday dinner table, too, so we can share the joy of a closely knit family.

The years are passing quickly, and although I know that day will come, we are all enjoying family life too much to give it up just yet. At twenty-two, Yana is attending community college where she's studying business, and is using her cosmetology license in her job at a beauty salon. Even before Yana could speak English, if a friend went into Yana's room, she'd come out with a new hairdo!

Kolya works at Chick-fil-A when he's not at his high school.

Rita is in her senior year of high school and working for a local veterinarian. She loves animals and wants to go into the veterinary care field.

Rick and I were meant to be the parents of these children and I would adopt again in a heartbeat. The journey has not always been easy, but it's been incredibly rewarding.

How we went from being a childless couple to a big family is one of those stories that could only happen with God's help.

~ Linda Landreth Phelps (as told to her by Fran Rahn)

ॐ 8 ॐ
A Husband's Devotion

An elderly woman, wearing a Santa hat, caught my attention. The man was talking to her about their home and someone coming to visit. I watched as she and her husband huddled together on the snack aisle of the Dollar Store. I hurried on to select my items. Later they stood in front of me at the checkout counter.

She picked up an item from the cart and turned toward me as if to leave the line. She seemed a little dazed.

In a quiet, calm voice, the gray haired man said, "Look at me."

She gazed up into his eyes.

"After you open a bag, you can't take it back," he said patiently.

Her head nodded. Silently, she returned the opened bag to the conveyor belt. A chip tumbled out. Before he could stop her, she picked it up and stuffed it into her mouth.

As it does with most children, the colorful, display shelf near the cash register enticed her. With a smile, she picked up a candy bar, held it tightly, and looked at her husband for approval.

"No, you can't get it. We have candy at home."

Obediently, she placed it back on the rack.

The distinguished looking man continued talking. "I bought a big candy bar and put it into the refrigerator. Now it's gone. I think Sam took it when he came over."

He spoke as though she could understand though he received little response. He looked at the cashier and asked, "Do you know where kangaroos eat?"

"At I-Hop," she answered with a grin as she rung up his items.

Despite the obvious difficulties the elderly gentleman experienced with the woman at his side, he retained his sense of humor and cheered up those around him.

I wondered what their lives had been like before her dementia. How long had he been her caregiver? Did she even know who he was? As the questions swirled in my head, sadness clutched my heart. Tears filled my eyes.

What kind of Christmas would they have? Would she anticipate it like a child does? Did she even remember Christmas?

As difficult as it was to watch their exchange, his devotion and patience also filled me with joy and encouragement. He presented her the gift of love knowing she probably couldn't reciprocate. What a perfect example of following Jesus' command to love.

- Rebecca Carpenter

My command is this: Love each other as I have loved you.

John 15:12 NIV

9
I Heard Him on the Roof

"There's no Santa Claus."
"There is, too. I heard him last Christmas."
"Silly. You heard Dad. I promise there's no Santa."

My two children hotly debated a topic near and dear to the hearts of many children around four or five. A part of each child wants to believe. After all, not believing might stop the annual flow of gifts. Continuing to believe can earn the label "baby" from more worldly friends and siblings.

While this conversation continued in a bedroom, my husband and my parents were nearby in the kitchen discussing how we could manage to change Santa's arrival from Christmas morning to tonight. There was the problem of making the change plausible to preschoolers. After we tossed around many ideas, we finally had a plan in place.

My mom went to talk to her grandchildren. "Kids, because we have the opportunity to visit Grandmommy and Granddaddy Van tomorrow, we are going to see if Santa can come tonight. While you get ready for your baths, I'll call the North Pole and talk to him."

Two children peeked around the corner to listen to her side of the conversation. "Oh, hello, Mrs. Claus. This is Teri and John's grandmother. Do you think it would be possible for Santa to bring their gifts tonight instead of in the morning? We've had a change of plans." (pause) "He's taking a shower? Yes, I'll be glad to wait while you ask him."

Several minutes passed as two wide-eyed children waited for an answer. I could almost hear them thinking, *Grandmother is talking to Santa!*

"Well hello, Santa. I didn't mean to get you out of the shower. I'd really appreciate it if you could come tonight so I can go to my family's get-together tomorrow. You can? That's great. We'll be expecting you. Thanks, again."

My mom hung up the phone and saw the children waiting around the corner. "Off you go, you two. You need to be ready for bed before Santa comes.

Meanwhile, David and my dad put their own plan into action. They climbed onto the roof as soon as Teri and John were sequestered in their baths. David, equipped with jingle bells, tapped on the roof to imitate several reindeer impatiently waiting to fly again while my dad bumped the inside of the chimney. I began putting gifts under the tree and in stockings. After what he thought an appropriate amount of time, my dad, in his most robust voice, bellowed, "Ho, Ho, Ho and a Merry Christmas to All. Goodnight!"

I turned around to find two astonished children standing in the hallway. "Mom, we heard Santa! He was on the roof with his reindeer!" exclaimed my son.

My daughter chimed in her agreement. "We even heard him coming down the chimney. Can we go look under the tree?"

I glanced toward the living room. "Let me check to see if Granddad has his camera ready, and then you may look."

The children entered the living room to find their dad and granddad looking no different than during any other ordinary evening.

The status of the Santa-doubtful suffered a severe loss that night. It was another year or two before my children were even fazed by the stories of their friends attempting to discredit Santa's existence.

Today when I tell the story to my grandchildren, I remind them that their parents didn't have to see Santa to believe he was real. The sounds on the roof and the toys under the tree were evidence enough. The story is a natural bridge toward telling them stories from my faith journey. I want them to understand there are times we believe even when we may only see the evidence with out hearts.

~ Carole A. Bell

10

Mustard Seeds and Cheap Perfume

He arrived at school on the first day with bare feet.

I was beginning third grade in the 1960s. Everybody knew getting a new pair of school shoes was necessary before the first day of school. Nevertheless, the tall boy with the kind, big brown eyes walked into our combination second/third grade classroom with feet that obviously had been toughened by outdoor play all summer as if they had never been in a pair of shoes.

I knew him from Vacation Bible School at our tiny country church. My grandmother, my mother, and other women in our church hauled kids in their cars to the two-week event. I had observed that he was always thoughtful of others during our refreshment and playtime. Just like his father, who resembled Abe Lincoln, he towered over the rest of us, yet he never used his size to get his way or bully other children.

My embarrassment and shock at his bare feet robbed me of politeness. I should have bounced off the bus and asked how his summer had been since VBS, but my shyness prevented that. However, I was never unkind to him and behaved in a friendly way — although I was a self-conscious little girl.

December rolled around. In those days, celebrating Christmas at school all month long was paramount. We created red and green construction paper chains for the cedar tree the high school boys in FFA (Future Farmers of America) had cut for our classroom. The sound of voices practicing Christmas songs for the Christmas Extravaganza filled the center hallway. Our little school burst with Christmas cheer.

In those days, classrooms had the drawing-of-names-day early in the month of December. We each scribbled our name on a white strip of paper and carefully folded it so no one would see even a letter. As the teacher passed around the container that held the names, each of us pulled out a strip. We were to buy a small gift for the person whose name we drew. Our teacher had instructed us to show no one except her as she called us individually to her desk. She glanced at our strip and recorded our name along with the name of the classmate we had drawn. She emphasized that we were not to exceed a predetermined monetary limit in our gift selection.

The last day of school before Christmas seemed to take forever to come. Finally, I woke up, dressed, ate breakfast, and boarded the bus with my gift for the student whose name I had drawn. The excitement over the day faded when I noticed my gift was from the boy who had started school with no shoes. It was now winter and he wore a pair of oversized scruffy boots.

I sat in the back of the classroom at my desk, carefully opening the gift — not knowing what to expect. He had selected for me a cheap perfume in a charming plastic decanter in the shape of an old-fashioned lamp with a detachable gold-colored shade. Then I was surprised to find a delicate necklace with a tiny cylindrical container filled with mustard seeds.

After shyly thanking him, I watched his Lincolnesque smile flash across his face. That gentle boy probably endured horrible teasing in his life as a student simply because his parents were poor. They were hardworking people who struggled to provide the basics. I am sure that even this simple gift was a big deal. Even though I was a child, I knew he and his family had made extra effort to purchase something that I would like. They knew my parents were people of faith and that I would understand the relevance of the mustard seed necklace.

Cheap perfume didn't matter to me as a little girl. I used it and recycled the lamp decanter for my sister and me to use when we played with our Barbie dolls. What style it added to a doll's living room!

Ironically, long after the chain had disappeared, I retained the miniscule, cylindrical container of mustard seeds. I often wore it around my neck, even into my college days, dangling from a circular wire, which was quite a popular neck accessory.

When I looked at the mustard seed, not only did I remember the biblical lesson of the mustard seed, but I also remembered the boy who gave it to me. My hope is that the gentle giant, who moved the next year from our community, learned to live his life to the fullest by having faith as a grain of mustard seed.

I had learned the lesson my parents modeled and taught me from the scripture, particularly the second chapter of James, in which the treatment of rich and poor people is discussed. James wrote in verse 1, *If you have faith in our glorious Lord Jesus Christ, you won't treat some people better than others.* (CEV)

The true message of Christmas is the Son of God laying aside his royalty, taking on human flesh, coming as the son of a poor young virgin, and giving his life so impoverished humans can be forgiven and share in his riches.

~ Bernadean J. Gates

≈ 11 ≈
Christmas Legacy

What began as a day of baking and decorating gingerbread man cookies with my toddler twenty-five years ago, became one of our family's most anticipated Christmas traditions

Today we continue to mix the dough, roll it out, and firmly press the cookie cutter into the dough to create the cutest little gingerbread men cookies. But now our intention is to do more than just eat them. Using a pin, we push a tiny hole through the top of each gingerbread man's head before we bake him. After he is baked, we insert an ornament hanger into the hole, decorate him with white icing, and hang him on the Christmas tree.

Not just one gingerbread man — dozens!

Along with other children's homemade ornaments, we hang so many gingerbread men on the tree, that we needed a separate tree to house all the gingerbread men. This tree, fondly known as the Cookie Tree, stands in the kitchen. My adult children look forward to not only making the cookies, but also reliving the memories.

But the best part is passing down the tradition to the next generation, and making and hanging cookies with my granddaughter.

Gingerbread men make yummy treats for cookie swaps, table decorations, and gifts, too.

Perhaps you can start a new tradition today. You never know…your tradition may become your legacy.

You'll find our recipe on the next page.

Gingerbread Men

½ cup butter
¾ cup sugar
1 egg
¼ cup molasses
Juice of ½ orange

3 ½ to 4 cups all-purpose flour
1 teaspoon baking soda
½ teaspoon salt
1 teaspoon ground cinnamon
1 teaspoon ground ginger

In a large mixing bowl, cream butter; gradually add sugar, beating until light and fluffy. Add egg, molasses, and orange juice; beat well. In a separate bowl, combine flour, soda, salt, and spices; add to creamed mixture, blending well. Divide dough in half; chill 1 hour or until stiff enough to handle. Roll out dough to ¼-inch thickness on a greased cookie sheet and use a gingerbread man cookie cutter to make the cookie. Remove the excess dough. Bake at 350 degrees for 10 minutes. Cool and decorate with Royal Icing.

Royal Icing

3 room-temperature egg whites
½ teaspoon cream of tartar
1 (16-ounce) package powdered sugar, sifted
Food coloring (if desired)

Beat egg whites and cream of tartar in a bowl until foamy; gradually add sugar. Beat 5-7 minutes. Icing dries quickly, so put plastic wrap over it.

Adapted from *Southern Living Cookbooks*. Copyright 1986 by Oxmoor House, Inc.

~ Debbie Presnell

❧ 12 ❧

Unexpected Guests for Christmas

No way! I said to myself when the pastor encouraged members of our church to invite someone lonely into our homes for Christmas. *I can't do another thing. I still have gifts to buy, and the house needs decorating. Surely the Lord understands that.*

As an afterthought I whispered, "Lord, if you want us to have someone over, you'll have to put it together."

He did.

One week before Christmas I answered the telephone.

"Hello, Geneba. This Shiroe."

"Ohhh," I recognized the accent of my husband's niece calling from Japan. "Chotto mate (Just a minute), I'll call Pete."

I hovered nearby as Pete spoke to her in Japanese. Finally, he paused and turned to me. "They want to come for Christmas. Is it okay?"

"Uhhh…yes. Sure," I said, reeling.

Shiroe's husband had drowned while fishing the summer before. Her ten-year-old son, Masao, and twelve-year-old daughter, Kana, struggled emotionally.

When they arrived two days later, I could see why they needed a vacation — especially Kana, who had been fishing with her dad when he drowned. Her sad eyes touched my heart.

Shiroe beamed as she unwrapped Oriental foods that my husband loves, sweet and salted fish with eyes that looked at me, and homemade miso (fermented soy beans). Aghast at the fish, I hid them in the refrigerator.

Masao loved American food: hot chocolate, pancakes and sweet rolls. Kana, however, didn't like anything American but cinnamon apple tea. I served her a lot of that. I'd do anything to bring a smile to her face. But, try as I did, she always looked wan.

Since the children spoke no English, and Shiroe spoke only a little, communication challenged us. Pete was constantly interpreting.

We learned early on that our guests loved shopping. Masao bought fishing gear, and Kana bought stuffed bears — lots of them. Sensing that she needed bear-hugs as well, I took every opportunity to hug her. She didn't respond and never spoke except to her mother and brother.

The day before Christmas, while I prepared dinner, I heard Shiroe coaching Masao. He came into the kitchen and said, "Something I help?"

I asked him to chop celery and cube bread for the stuffing. When it was time to fill the turkey, Kana finally smiled as they spooned stuffing into the bird.

The previous summer, I had bought a piñata on sale — a pig. Pete tied it from a living room beam, and after the candlelight service at church, we took turns trying to break it. Masao, much to his glee, struck the mighty blow that sent the candies flying.

The next day, Christmas, we drove to our cabin near the Oregon Coast. Pete and I hoped to show our guests the lighthouses, clean beaches, and wild surf, but the day after Christmas was rainy. So, I took them shopping. Nothing could have pleased them more.

Tillamook's largest store is a Fred Meyer. It sells everything from groceries to sporting goods. I bought some discounted Christmas wrap. But my guests shopped and shopped and shopped. Shiroe bought gifts for all the Japanese relatives. The children bought gifts for all their classmates.

Then I took them to Tillamook Cheese Factory. We toured the factory, purchased items in the gift shop, and bought the largest ice cream cones they had ever seen. Shiroe, however, had forgotten something she wanted to buy at Fred Meyer, so we returned. She made the purchase, and we were back in the car ready to return to the cabin, when she said, "Geneba, Kana want buy a bear at cheese factory." I sighed and turned the car around.

The next day the rain had passed, and we planned to show our guests the beauties of the Oregon Coast before heading home. But as Shiroe and I prepared breakfast, she said we needed to return to Fred Meyer. "Masao want buy fishing reel."

Exasperated, I replied, "We have a Fred Meyer in Oregon City. We can go tomorrow."

"Masao worry they not have same one." Shiroe waited a moment, then took a deep breath and continued. "Kana want go cheese factory. Want another bear."

"Another bear?" I rolled my eyes at Pete as he came through the room. "Why?"

"Yesterday, bear girl. Now, want boy."

I sighed. There was no fighting it. They might never return to America.

While we drove around Cape Meares to show them the spectacular views of the ocean, the children hardly looked. Not until we returned to Tillamook did they come alive. Masao hurried into Fred Meyer, and all of them did another round of shopping.

At Tillamook Cheese, Kana bought her bear. Shiroe bought another large bag of gifts from the sale tables. I insisted on ice cream.

The next day, in Oregon City, I decided to show them the local sights. We ate lunch at McDonalds. The children wanted to see whether an American hamburger tasted better than those they bought in Japan. I took pictures of them happily munching on burgers and fries.

Then we went for a walk along the bluff above the Willamette River. The temperature dipped, and the light rain became snow. I walked along beside Kana. Shiroe and Masao followed. On impulse, I caught Kana's hand in mine. Though she didn't show it, I sensed her pleasure. I swung our hands back and forth as if we were both schoolgirls, and I knew in that moment that all the efforts had made a difference for her.

"Geneba," Shiroe called. We turned, and she snapped our picture. She handed the camera to Masao and grabbed Kana's other hand for another photo.

That evening when I went downstairs to tell them goodnight, Shiroe asked me to pray with her and the children. Emotion overcame me as I prayed for God's blessing on them. I sensed that their load of grief had lightened. They would take the love we'd shared back to Japan.

The last day, Shiroe packed. They had bought gifts for over a hundred friends, classmates and relatives. I'll never know how she stuffed all their purchases, including Kana's ten bears, in only seven bags.

We were running late when we headed toward airport security. Even so, Shiroe eyed the airport shops longingly. We waved as they disappeared through the gate. Shiroe popped her head back through to get one more look at us, and we waved again.

Pete and I looked at each other and grinned. No, it wasn't our usual Christmas, but we'd shared it, and God made it one of our best.

~ Geneva Cobb Iijima

❧ 13 ☙
An M&M Christmas

A big part of Christmas is remembering past Christmas blessings. Yes, many families, including our own, have suffered hardships that make the season hurt in one way or another, but just about everybody has at least one positive memory of Christmas worth recalling.

Sometimes we need a little help in the remembering. Times are tough and that is why I suggest keeping a decorated dish, filled with M&M candies, in the living room for all to see and sample. Why? Because of the letter *M* on each colorful round piece.

The M reminds me of the Christmas M's. Like Messiah, Mary, Manger… and Magic. But not the hocus-pocus kind. The real Magic of pure, unadulterated Joy.

When I was a child, Magic was everywhere — in the decorations, the homemade cookies we helped decorate, the carols and the anticipation of what we might find under the tree. We always had a live tree that smelled of woods and wonder. We sang carols around the piano. We put up a manger and spent hours arranging and rearranging the cows, sheep, and shepherds until the scene was just right.

We didn't go to the mall, nor did we expect a mountain of presents. Christmas was about two things only: celebrating Baby Jesus' birthday, and being with loved ones. Now as an adult, although I enjoy all the decorating and baking, I find the Magic, not in the carols and lights, but in the Miracle.

Often, something is missing in the celebration of Christmas. Turn on the television, and we are bombarded with Midnight Madness sales and the latest, greatest electronic gadgets. What has happened to Magic, Memories and Miracles? We need to be reminded of them during this blessed season.

One way to do this is to use that dish of M&Ms to remember all the M's of Christmas: Messiah, Mary, Mother, Manger, Memories, Meals, Magi, Midnight and Mystery.

Oh, and don't forget Magic. The Magic of the Miracle.

~ *Theresa Jenner Garrido*

Even though you do not believe me, believe the miracles, that you may know and understand that the Father is in me and I in the Father.

John 10:38 NIV

14

The Sparkling Bow of Joy

The doorbell rang a few weeks before Christmas. "C'mon, I'll walk with you," my neighbor said, "the gals are waiting."

Gathering with my neighbors to create decorations had been one of the activities I had enjoyed during the Christmas season. But not anymore. With my eyesight gone and my physical world dark, my equally bleak attitude robbed the the season of its joy.

"I think I'll stay home this time," I said.

So much I needed to do, to accomplish, to live for, had all vanished. All wiped away by the retinal disease that robbed me of my eyesight just a few months prior.

Tears flowed with each step of the painful adjustment.

"Mommy, can I have a peanut butter and jelly sandwich?" my five-year-old called out from the kitchen.

A simple task, but now, groping to find the pantry and the items in it wasn't that easy. Trying to determine jars or cans from one another increased my frustration. Anxiety cramped my stomach as I feared I couldn't be a normal mommy to my three-, five-, and seven-year-old sons.

The Christmas season multiplied the tasks to accomplish. I had to try harder to squelch the turmoil inside. While following the routine, I fumbled with apparent resignation, but inside I still longed to have even a tiny bit of eyesight.

I'd be satisfied with the miniscule amount of sight I'd had just the Christmas before. It had allowed me to distinguish their facial expressions and the sparkle in my children's eyes when they opened their gifts.

But this Christmas, I saw a gray nothing — no red or green, no colors, no shadows. Nothing.

Although reluctant, I accompanied my husband, Gene, on shopping trips. I held onto the shopping cart and he pulled it through crowded aisles.

"Look at that," he said. "Jeff would love that."

I smiled and looked in his direction.

"Honey, I'm sorry," he said.

I shrugged. "Hey, I forget too."

But I never forgot. The truth was that time and time again, out of habit, I glanced in the direction of the object, but with no retina function, my brain didn't register anything. That part of my life was painfully empty…as empty as the shopping cart seemed to me.

Then, one cold morning in December, I inhaled a long breath and vowed that this upcoming Christmas season would be the one where I would conquer my emotions and follow through with the usual holiday tasks. I lined up all the boxes holding decorations against the wall.

"Okay, guys, who wants to watch a movie?" Gene rounded up our sons, giving me the time to arrange the decorations.

"You go with Daddy," I said, "and maybe I'll have some cookies for you later."

Months of practice made baking easier, the burning episodes less frequent, and mistakes like using flour for powdered sugar also a thing of the past. I navigated through the kitchen with relative ease. Even doing laundry and cleaning became simpler each time I did them. Barefoot, I could tell which spots I'd missed while sweeping the kitchen floor.

I reached into the storage boxes filled with Christmas treasures, and the moment my fingers touched an item, the shape and texture told me what it was. Since I'd seen it while sighted, memories of its color painted the item in my mind. I decorated each area of the house, left the tree decorations as a task for our sons, and placing the star atop the Christmas tree as the job for Gene.

I raised the volume of "Silent Night" on the stereo and sunk onto the sofa. The silence of my darkness suddenly had a soothing melody of contentment. And I had learned to push back those nagging moments of nostalgia of days with sight.

Christmas morning came quickly, and I heard the high-pitched voices of our sons outside our bedroom door. They came in and rushed to our bed. "Guys, get up, we want to open presents."

Each voice had a distinct sound and I could tell their mood by the inflection and tone. They jumped, giggled, and teased each other as I wiped the sleep from my eyes.

I reached for my robe and held out my hand, "C'mon, let's see what Santa brought."

Leading me by the hand was normal for them. But this time, they rushed out the door and headed toward the Christmas tree in our family room.

I followed the familiar path to the couch. A fresh pine scent wafted through, and bells on the tree chimed as they lifted packages to find one to open.

"Let's take turns," their daddy said. "And don't forget to tell Mommy what you got."

I sighed inwardly. My husband's thoughtfulness warmed my heart, but following that instruction would be difficult in the midst of their excitement.

"Look what I got." Joe ripped wrapping paper and placed it on my lap.

I reached out my hand. "Show your Mommy."

But it wasn't the gift I wanted to see, but their expressions of delight that matched their words. I longed to see the sparkle in their eyes when they opened what they had asked for all year long.

That's when I realized that dwelling on what I couldn't see threatened to erase the Christmas joy. I fought the temptation to sink into self-pity, and swallowed hard to keep the tears inside.

My husband appeared behind me on the couch and whispered in my ear, "Are you okay?"

I nodded. "I'll be back."

I rose from the couch and groped my way to the bedroom. I sat on the bed and chided myself for being unable to handle this time with our family.

I had been so strong, had faced tough moments with courage, but now… why the sadness, the anguish and impatience?

I couldn't understand. With a tissue, I pressed my eyes and sobs poured out.

My husband slid beside me on the bed. "What can I do for you?"

His sweetness and warmth further emphasized my sorrow. I was disappointing him, causing an added burden for him. With emotional distress, I'd failed in my role as a wife to him and a mom to my sons.

And when anguish nearly overwhelmed me, I suppressed one last sob and looked up. "God, help me to have the courage and strength I need."

"This is the best present yet!" one of our sons cried out.

I held my breath and paused for a few moments. My son's words brought a sobering truth that opened the eyes of my heart. His gift delighted him. But I had missed mine, overlooking and disregarding my greatest present — the one that filled the emptiness of my dark world. It was in the family room — it sang to me with little voices, with little arms that hugged me, and with the sweetest melody of each "I love you, Mommy."

I stuffed the wrinkled tissue in my pocket and reached for Gene's hand. "Let's go. I don't want to miss a minute of this."

I had asked God to help me cope. But rather than just coping, he taught me to enjoy what lies beyond physical sight, what the warmth of love offers and what truly holds meaning and purpose.

Years have passed, and in the midst of enjoyment and laughter with my neighbors, I create better Christmas decorations. I decorate my days with sparkles of hope, placing red and green ribbons around the joy Jesus brings, around his promise of peace.

Equipped to care for my family, I wait with anticipation for each Christmas where the gift of their love delights the eyes of my heart, and places a sparkling bow that reflects the gratitude that shines in my heart.

- Janet Perez Eckles

❧ 15 ❦
When the Most Wonderful Time of the Year Isn't

For me, it was 2004.

I stared at the blinking lights on our Christmas tree, almost in a trance-like state. It wasn't the colors or the tree. I was shell shocked at how fast my life had changed and how much those I loved suffered.

In a year, both my husband and I had job changes. My husband's job was such a transition we had moved 300 miles away. We knew no one.

Our toddler was recovering from a horrendous first year where we nearly lost her. She needed therapy several times a week in addition to medical appointments.

My dad had passed away. When he got the diagnosis he knew the outcome even though for months he didn't even appear sick. The strapping man who reminded me of John Wayne was gone.

Celebrate Christmas?

I was having trouble finding reasons to get out of bed each morning. That year had been full of heartbreak for so many I know online and in person. So much transition, sickness and death. Job loss. Injustices. Broken marriages. Miscarriages. Widowhood. All that, without my even looking at newspaper headlines or listening to television news. And I knew there were families grieving from suicides. Shootings.

Life seems full of bad news. But the song says it's the most wonderful time. How can that be? How can anyone celebrate the season when there is no feeling? When everything is numb and time feels frozen?

- **I know for me, it helped to decorate.** That was my way of not only remembering I had two children who needed the bright lights and Christmas music, it was also a statement. I was down, but I refused to be out. I felt like the devil's plan was to destroy everything in and around me and if I gave in, he won. Even if it was one small thing I did to remember it was Christmas, I was bound and determined.

- **I also thought of others.** It wasn't easy because I felt so lost inside myself. My favorite thing to do is to have blank cards and point to a random name in the phone book. I write something like, "You mean so much to God that I pointed to a name in a phone book to send a card and the person is you. You are not forgotten. You are loved. Have a Merry Christmas." I don't sign my name or leave a return address. I want them blessed, and it takes my mind off my situation to know I'm encouraging someone else.
- **If I couldn't take the upbeat Christmas music, I put praise music on.** If the words, as Christian and biblical as I needed them to be were heartbreaking to hear, I played instrumental music.
- **I wish I'd been more honest.** There were some events I shouldn't have attended but didn't want to let anyone down. Other times I isolated myself and should have said something. Keeping it all in isn't healthy; it plays right into the enemy's hand. We don't have to air all our laundry, just say we're struggling and can use prayer. And when someone offers, we should let them.

Since then, I've had other difficult Christmas seasons but nothing close to that one in 2004. I think a lot of why I was able to bounce back a little faster was I applied the suggestions above and realized the pain had purpose. Hosea 2:14 has been my lifeline in dark times and I want my adversity to mean something and help someone else.

My prayer is that if you're struggling this Christmas, something here will help you.

Father, let every person reading this feel your presence right now, and in the days and weeks to come. For every event and circumstance that has robbed them of peace and joy, replace it multifold with blessings we can't define. Give them special moments that are your love notes just for them. Give them strength to celebrate Christmas, even if it's in a different way this year. Draw them close to you. We give you the glory, honor and praise. In Jesus' name, Amen.

~ Julie Arduini

16

The Light

"Hurry, or we'll be late." My parents seemed to be taking forever to get ready for my first school Christmas party. As a six-year-old, I could hardly wait to get there. The older school children had told me there would be presents from Santa. Earlier in the week, I had helped my classmates cut construction paper and paste it into chains and also threaded popcorn onto string making white ropes for tree decorations. Some of the students memorized poems and readings to recite in the program.

When my parents, younger brother and I arrived at the one-room country school, light shone through the windows showing off the paper snowflakes that the students had made. Several cars were already parked on the school grounds.

"Good evening. Glad you could come." My teacher welcomed us as we walked into the building.

"Oh wow, look at the tree! Please, may I go see?" I begged my parents. The Christmas tree sat on the side of the stage and had been decorated after the closing of the school day. It glowed with various colored electric bubble lights. A wrapped present for each child waited under the large pine tree. The paper and popcorn chains now encircled the tree. Tinsel danced as it dangled from the pine needles. Candy canes hung on the branches. An angel sat on the top.

Liquid bubbled up and down inside each light and shown through the colored-glass candles. I was enthralled by this new sight, having never seen anything so pretty and unique. The rest of the evening paled in comparison to the lovely bubble lights. I couldn't keep my eyes off their glowing beauty.

After a few years, my parents purchased bubble lights for our family's use. My siblings and friends enjoyed their exotic illumination. When my parents decorated the tree, we watched with fascination to witness the bubbling beauty.

"Let's go buy some bubble lights for our tree," I suggested to Helen, my new wife, the first Christmas after our marriage. Through the years, I have carefully placed the bubble lights on the tree where everyone can admire them. Then Helen adds the rest of the decorations to accent the colorful bubbly lights.

The popularity of bubble lights on holiday trees has decreased throughout the years, but I still think they are the prettiest of any Christmas lights. I buy replacements at yard sales when people are getting rid of theirs. Even after sixty-five years, I continue to show the lights to our family and friends and enjoy telling about the first time I saw the unusual lights.

Thirty years after I first encountered the fascinating lights, I encountered "The Light" when I accepted Jesus as my Savior. The moving colored lights had drawn me to examine them closely. Christ drew me by his love, grace and forgiveness. Now, the pretty bubble lights pale in comparison with The Light that lives in my heart.

Seeing the Christmas lights is a favorite for many people, but soon they are taken down until another year. The Light they represent, though, is with us all year long to guide and help along life's pathway.

Christ is the best light anyone can have.

~ Larry C. Hoover

Jesus said to the people, "I am the light of the world.
If you follow me, you won't be stumbling through the darkness,
because you will have the light that leads to life."

John 8:12 NLT

17

Picture Perfect Christmas

When my dad died in 2013, I knew many changes were in the future for our family. Many hurdles to be faced would be holidays. How can a celebration ever be the same when someone is missing? There would be birthdays, Father's Days, anniversaries. My parents' sixty-first wedding anniversary would have been on New Year's Eve that year.

After Dad's death, I knew that first Christmas without him would be the hardest for Mom. I didn't want her to be alone when she woke up that holiday morning. Although my brother, Tim, was there, I knew the house would feel empty without her longtime mate.

My husband and I arrived a few days before December 25. We brought gifts and piled them under the tree. We did the cooking and watched Christmas movies. We ate popcorn, made cookies, read holiday cards, and wrapped more gifts. We admired the wooden ornaments on the tree, skillfully made by Dad with his scroll saw. We tried to behave as if there was not a huge presence missing from our family.

Christmas day arrived and the activity of the household seemed subdued as we went through the ritual of morning greetings, coffee, breakfast, and then gathered around the tree. Tim handed out gifts between making trips back to his camera, which was poised on a tripod for the usual pictorial recording. We each had our usual places to sit in favorite chairs, next to the fireplace, or on the floor. Noticeably empty was Dad's space at the end of the sofa.

Paper ripped, bows were torn, and oohs and aahs transpired while we admired each other's new possessions. All the packages had been unwrapped — except one. A large rectangular gift stood against the wall in red and green paper.

My brother handed the box to Mom. After tearing through the paper, she reached inside the box and ran her hands against the surface of its contents. Tears filled her eyes and tightness formed in my throat when she lifted up a painting of Dad.

It wasn't a new portrait. It had been stored in their home for years. It was older than my parents' marriage. When my dad served in the Navy in the early 1950's, an artist friend had painted the portrait. Dad had mailed the rolled up canvas home to Mom while they were engaged.

Of course, she loved the artistic treasure, but Dad was always too embarrassed to let her hang it on the wall in the house. He thought it would appear as if he thought too highly of himself.

After more than a half century of being stored, some of the paint had chipped, the color had faded, and it needed a frame. Restoring this old painting became my brother's present to our mother that Christmas. He couldn't have chosen a better gift in any store on the face of the earth.

Now, whenever anyone walks into the house, Dad's portrait graces the living room wall. Not because he thought so highly of himself, but because we think so highly of him.

That Christmas present changed everything. Not only did we feel Dad's presence by having the picture of him, young and healthy, we had a renewed presence of what Christmas was all about.

Our celebrating the birth of Jesus took on a renewed meaning. God sent Jesus to restore us from being hidden away, chipped, broken, faded. He gave his life to give us new life. Now when I see that picture I am reminded not of death and loss, but of restoration and joy.

~ Barbara Latta

18

The Question

"Dad, if I wasn't here with you, would you still put out the Christmas decorations?" my daughter asked as we began to put up the Christmas tree.

We started about a month earlier than usual so we could enjoy the tree, lights, and decorations longer than in previous years. It's our favorite pastime to turn off the house lights and sit in the darkened room watching the rhythmic pulse of the tree lights. It can be quite peaceful, if not a little hypnotic. Add the roaring fireplace casting its dancing brilliance on the light show and…ahh, one of the beautiful moments of the Christmas season.

God used my daughter's question to speak to my heart. Why do I wait for the majority of the year to get into the holiday spirit? You know the one I'm talking about.

We slow down a bit from our hectic schedules and become more nostalgic.
We remember the good times of past holiday gatherings with extended family.
We reach out to friends with whom we've lost contact over the year.
There's an expectant excitement in the air.
Fresh baked pies, bread, and cookies create that inviting smell of "home."
Life seems to take on a softer hue as the Christmas season approaches.
Again the question — would I still…celebrate?

Why do I wait until the holiday season to express my feelings to loved ones, to appreciate my friends, to be grateful for God's multiplied blessings in my life? If my daughter wasn't home, would I even bother to go through the trouble of hauling out all the decorations only to take it all down, box it up, and put it back in storage?

God is God all year round, and he sent us Christ, bundled in swaddling clothes and lying in a manger. To most folks, he seemed ordinary, but he was far from ordinary. Christ was the most beautiful and indescribable gift God could have given us. His perfect son. His perfect love. So instead of saving that "special feeling" for the end of the year, we should celebrate God all year long!

God, thank you for who you are and for your countless blessings! Awaken in us today a sense of your constant presence and a mesmerizing wonder of your continuing goodness!

~ Nate Stevens

Thanks be to God for His indescribable gift!

2 Corinthians 9:15 NKJV

19
A Flash of Red

Glittered cards in an array of colors adorned the wall in my daughter's room. The small tree from the mountains of western North Carolina held its place in the corner, wafting a sweet fragrance of balsam throughout the space.

This room wasn't situated in her lovely newlywed home, the one the young couple had dreamed of and saved for, or the one I'd helped decorate. It was one of many rooms that lined the hall of a hospital cancer ward four floors up. Brooke was thirty-three and battling late stage breast cancer. It was a diagnosis that caught both her doctors and our family by surprise.

One late afternoon while sitting by her bedside, relieving her husband for a dinner break, I silently prayed for strength as I lovingly watched over her failing body. This mother's heart was breaking.

Bald from repeated chemotherapy and radiation, Brooke's pale face sat in stark contrast to the bright, multicolored tree bulbs blinking through strands of tinsel. Only her bright eyes could rival the lights on the tree.

Brooke turned to me, a tinge of pink highlighting her cheeks. "Mom," she said, "the most beautiful cardinal sat on my windowsill. After the longest time he turned to me as if he was saying, 'One day you will fly,' then he flew away in a flash of red."

Before the following Christmas, Brooke, too, would fly heavenward in what seemed like a flash.

I gathered my things from her home and traveled to mine, several hours away, to my husband and ninety-five-year-old mother, who suffered from dementia.

Weeks later, as a new Christmas season approached, I found myself exhausted and raw with grief. I had neither the strength nor the desire to decorate another room with blinking bulbs and tinsel. After all, I'd just said goodbye to the brightest light I'd known for thirty-three years.

"Are you not putting up a tree this year?" my mother asked, only days before Christmas.

Knowing this would probably be Mother's last Christmas, I pushed through my grief and gathered a few boxes of decorations for a tabletop tree. This wasn't the tall live tree that normally graced our home but one hastily bought at a dollar store. The important thing was that mother thought it was beautiful. I sometimes envied the happy little world she now lived in.

A few days after I'd put up the artificial tree, a package arrived by mail. Inside the pretty wrapped box was a hand-carved ornament. It wasn't just any ornament but one in the shape of a cardinal. The wooden treasure was from a dear friend who had made ornaments for our family for years. Inside the box was a note. I read the words, "I felt led by God to carve the little bird this year — as if He was guiding my hands."

I had not shared Brooke's conversation about the cardinal on her hospital window ledge with anyone. Tears ran down my face as I held the beautiful bird close to my heart. I saw Brooke's face that day in the hospital, at peace with the knowledge she would soon see her Savior and Lord. To her, the cardinal was a harbinger of heaven.

Each year the cardinal holds a place of honor on our tree. It reminds me that Christmas comes in many ways. Sometimes, even in a flash of red.

~ Dee Dee Parker

❧ 20 ☙
Plug-ins

In Old Town Sacramento a souvenir shop was going out of business just before the Christmas season. I dragged myself inside hoping to find a bargain, or at least something to brighten up the holidays, which at times hadn't always been merry for me. The souvenir shop sat within the façade of building fronts simulating an 1800's western town. Restaurants, banks and saloon signs prominently hung outside each old establishment.

The shop's interior seemed to envelope me in its rugged charm, housing tree ornaments, tins, picture frames, and hand-crafted pillows and aprons. It was narrow walled, with one long, broad aisle down its center. Sawdust chips lay neatly scattered across the wooden floorboards. Cinnamon scented candles and bars of handmade soaps sat layered atop silver display trays and glass shelves. A whiff of fresh molten saltwater taffy from a nearby candy vendor drifted in on a sweet breeze.

I became even more enchanted near the back of the shop, because that's where I met my brand new porcelain angel — the only one of her kind. Her face, a shade of smooth dark chocolate, was surrounded by a mass of tiny jet-black curls. Her white taffeta gown with a lace-trimmed overlay was illuminated from underneath by small lights. The miniature candlestick she held in her delicate little right hand lit up too, casting a warm light across her face. Even with the discount she seemed a bit pricey, but the investment might well be worth the cost for her to sit atop my Christmas tree. Over the years, I had switched to angels, instead of stars to adorn the top of our tree each year.

However, after arriving home, I discovered my new angel had a short somewhere in her circuitry, and I couldn't pinpoint the source. When I plugged the end of the cord into the electric socket, her dress, or her candle, sometimes both, failed to light up. I considered taking her back to the shop and ask for a refund, but it was near closing time and she was a clearance item. Besides, she was too beautiful, too unique to give up anyway. Maybe I'd never find another quite like her or at reduced price either.

So every year thereafter, I simply hoisted her up onto the tree top, forgetting all about how she once lit up. Searching for faulty wiring inside would take time, and it might make matters worse. Trying to "plug-in" wasn't worth the effort anymore. I imagined all I'd get was a continued lack of connectivity, no energy, no light, a fleeting beauty no longer bright.

That's the kind of feeling I'd had in the past when going through times of what seemed like spiritual darkness in my life. The dark voice of isolation would intrude into my thoughts. *No one wants to hear your problems…yours aren't nearly as important as other people's issues…who wants to be around you right now anyway?"* Isolation just seemed easier.

Several years after having purchased my angel, and during a particularly stressful Christmas season, my holiday spirit was waning and light of any kind was hard to find. Illnesses, disappointment, and sad memories clouded each day.

That year, even my chimney sweeper had bad news. "You've got a big problem, ma'am. Your base plate has a huge crack in it. In fact, the chicken wire beneath the cornerstone is starting to show. It could start a house fire. It'll cost about $350.00 to repair."

He wrote on my receipt in big bold letters of blue ink: DO NOT USE! He charged me $129 for the cleaning anyway. So I couldn't light up my fireplace either. But I dragged on with must-do holiday chores, still feeling lonely and alone.

On Christmas Eve morning I sat sipping coffee in my dim living room before heading out to my last work day of the year. I decided to at least remove the porcelain angel from her plastic storage encasement. She'd been lying there inside it on the table, face up but ignored all the previous week. I took her out, dusted her dress and lifted her up to the customary position atop the Christmas tree I'd hastily decorated earlier that week. I decided just for old time's sake to try plugging her in once again.

Somehow, as if with renewed energy and power, the magnificent brilliance reappeared, and it startled me. There my angel stood in all her previous glory, bright, beautiful, and illuminated like never before! A brief tug on the tiny candle bulb in her hand caused it to light up again too. A purely good and lovely feeling spread through me. It seemed to come up from somewhere deep down inside, from a place where no one but God can see and enlighten, and it felt wonderful. There was no more darkness or isolation for either my angel…or me.

I left for work that morning thinking how much I love my angel, both when we first met and then the day she decided to light up again, years later. She had showed up just when I needed her most. She reminded me of what is so easy to forget whenever I'm feeling sad, confused and overwhelmed.

I've learned that I had to keep plugging in my angel to a source of light before she could shine once again. I've since found that I must continually seek the only One who understands my needs, my worries, and can brighten a Christmas angel or tune out the voice of isolation.

I must keep looking to the power that is always there, no matter how dark things may seem. I must keep *plugging-in* again and again, knowing the light will come at the right time.

~ *Carlitta Cole-Kelly*

21

Christmas Presence

We all looked forward to Christmas 2008 with unmatched enthusiasm. But even at that, my nephew Matt was ahead of the pack. It had been a grueling struggle since April when leukemia swept Matt, only twenty-eight years old, into its crushing grip.

We muddled through Easter absorbing the shock of it. After all, this couldn't be possible in our family. This is the kind of stuff that happens to other families. The kind of families you read about in the newspaper and encounter through co-workers and classmates. But this kind of tragedy definitely does not happen in our family.

Except this time, it did.

Our annual Memorial Day cookout ended on a somber note as Matt headed for the hospital and an intense round of chemotherapy in preparation for a stem cell transplant. Heartbreaking barely describes what it felt like watching two little boys cling to their daddy for the want of understanding why he had to leave them behind. But go away he did.

Meghan, his wife, stood by managing daily visits to the hospital, her part-time job, and keeping their sons occupied. Five-year-old Anthony and three-year-old Doug made get well cards for their daddy.

On the 4th of July, firecrackers exploded in brilliant streams of red, white and blue outside Matt's hospital room. He watched from the window and waited for the blood test result that would give us a green light for his stem cell transplant.

Labor Day passed. More waiting. Finally in mid-September the stem cell transplant was scheduled and at last we breathed a sigh of relief. Matt's stem cell procedure brought the hope of a full recovery. He referred to the date of his transplant as his new birthday.

Thanksgiving arrived and Matt's recovery sprinted to the top of everyone's list of things for which we were truly thankful. It was wonderful to watch him grow stronger every day. One blood test after another brought us encouraging news. No cancer. No cancer. No cancer.

When we all gathered on Christmas day, the presents were piled high around the tree but they were not the main event. Nothing in Santa's sack compared with the joy of having Matt with us after surviving such life-threatening circumstances.

The moment Matt and his family walked through the door, Christmas in all its resplendent glory shone brightly in the warmth of his broad smile. Just as they stepped inside, Anthony and Doug, squealing merrily, headed straight to the family room to join their cousins and see what Santa brought. We were all together in the same house. Christmas had arrived.

Except for his bald head, discretely concealed under a Santa cap, Matt was a robust picture of good health. All day long he played with the children, feasted on his favorite foods, laughed, relaxed, and celebrated. Though I managed to join in the fun, mostly I just sat back and observed him enjoying his favorite role as husband and dad, and relishing every moment of it.

At one point I looked across the room and raised my glass to Matt. He winked at me and smiled, raising his glass in return, saying, "Merry Christmas Aunt Annie! Life is good."

"It sure is Matt," I replied. "It sure is." Never was life so good in our family as it was that very moment.

The turn of the calendar page to a new year brought us renewed hope for the future. Until the second week of January 2009 when a routine blood test revealed that the cancer had returned with a vengeance. How could someone who looked so healthy just three weeks before, be facing this nightmare yet again? And this time with diminished options?

Matt took up his battle as determined and courageous as ever, his family standing by him with fierce love and devotion. And the seasons passed again while one experimental avenue of treatment after another lead nowhere.

By Christmas 2009 Matt was hospitalized again and was hardly recognizable as the strapping young husband and father whose return to good health we had toasted just one year prior. On Christmas Day when my husband and I went to see him, Matt was no longer able to speak but the ever-present warmth in his eyes made words unnecessary. Matt was grateful for every finger that was lifted on his behalf. Never once through the many months of treatment he received, did I ever see his lips shy to form the words "thank you" to all who crossed his path.

When it was time for us to leave, Matt, who could barely raise his head off the pillow, reached to shake my husband's hand and thank us for coming to visit. His warm wonderful eyes pierced my heart straight through.

On January 6, 2010, Matt passed away.

It has been a heart-wrenching challenge learning to live without him. But his spirit is strong and shines brilliantly through the tender embrace of Anthony and Doug. As I look back on those days, especially after Matt passed away, I am amazed at the strength and grace with which Meghan processed her profound loss and found the courage to carry on.

Matt's imprint on our lives will be everlasting. That Christmas of 2008 remains one of my favorite memories.

My niece will be making some new Christmas memories this year. By God's good grace Meghan and Andy have found each other. He is a fine and loving young man and they will marry in the year to come.

Matt's presence is felt at Christmas and at all of our family gatherings. His spirit is an integral force within each of us that propels us into the future armed with a measure of his courage, hope and determination — the gifts that keep on giving.

~ Annmarie B. Tait

❧ 22 ❦
The Story

Each year I look for the supernatural in Advent like a magician pulling a rabbit from a hat, thinking that if I say the right words or do the right activity, I'll be able to conjure up the true meaning of Christmas and — dare I say? — a super spiritual status. I look for that hidden Narnia-like door into the Nativity.

This frenzied need to find and create the perfect spiritual experience has not always been part of my Christmas celebration. When I was a child, Advent was simple. There were no internet resources dictating how to celebrate the incarnate God, how to ponder anew the humble entrance of the King in five easy steps, how to shut-out consumerism.

In our house, there were only family, candles, and the Story — and we didn't even use the traditional pink and purple candles. (I still don't today.) We had the same red and green pillar candles year after year, sitting in the same place atop the half-wall divider between dining room and living room. They were the sacred sentries keeping watch over dinner and television activities, present wrapping and holiday baking.

Each year was the same. We lit a candle. We read part of the Christmas story. We acted it out. We acted it out again — enough times so each person could play each role. As children, we liked that predictability, the simplicity of it.

I remember the pink wooden doll bed we used for a manger, and the green and white knit blanket we used for swaddling clothes, a blanket that had wrapped me warm as a baby. I remember my dad in his maroon bathrobe as a shepherd. I remember singing "We Three Kings" as the kings marched down the hallway, my sister's voice always the loudest.

And I remember the Spirit illustrating Jesus' Story through us. We had become more than passive recipients of the timeless account. We had become witnesses to it. Bearers of the Good News.

We were children, acting simple parts, and yet our worship at the manger was more than a charade. We may have been dressed as a young, frightened girl from Nazareth, or a rich wise sage, but the knees we bowed before the Christ child were our own. In a mysterious way, we were shepherds, watching diligently over our daily activities of sports and homework. And just as those first Bethlehem shepherds made their choice to journey to the manger, we chose to journey and see, to leave behind the mundane for the profound, even if for only twenty minutes of retelling the Story.

So now, when Advent comes around, what do I want to do with my children? Light a candle. Read part of the Story. Enter in through action.

What do I gain from shouting into a darkened living room the words of the angel, "Do not be afraid. I bring you good news of great joy that will be for all the people"? Or by jealously sneering the words of King Herod, "Go and make a careful search for the child. As soon as you find him, report to me, so that I too may go and worship him."

I gain perspective. I realize the Herod-like parts of my own heart that have ulterior motives.

I gain glory. I wonder at the amazement of the shepherds as they hear first that the Savior of the world has made an obscure entrance.

I gain commitment as I say, "I am the Lord's servant. May it be to me as you have said."

I gain faith as I receive the words, "Nothing is impossible with God."

Although my children are far from stellar dramatists, they know how to pretend, to create story, to dress up. After all, Jesus called the children to come to him.

How better to come than entering into the Story, his coming.

~ Sondra Kraak

23

Christmas Potpourri

Each year in late October I manage to persuade my husband to take me to the mountains for my birthday. During our several hikes I gather enough treasure to fill a large bucket or cardboard box to take home to Florida.

The mix of deep-ridged tree bark, tiny pine cones, acorns, seed pods — and yes, even a few huge river rocks — usually leaves my hubby with the question, "How…and why…are we taking this heavy concoction on a six hundred mile trek when we have magnolia pods, berries, and tons of other woodsy stuff in our own backyard?"

This year I look up at him with my hands on my hips, ready for battle. I'm just over five feet tall. He's six feet, six inches. I retort, "I don't understand why *you* don't understand me." And we playfully banter back and forth.

I wonder if he really knows I love how he pretends to be annoyed and does this eye-rolling thing and then smiles at me before he answers with something not so funny, like, "You know, I wonder that too."

"Very funny, Dennis," I say. "You know I've waited all year to finally get a chance to wear my suede boots. While we walk hand-in-hand down steep rocky trails all summer, I imagine the frigid mountain wind blowing through my hair. So let's thank God we're not roasting in the tropical oven we call Central Florida on this beautiful autumn weekend."

Then I start to hum and sing the line of a classic song. "Isn't it romantic?… La, la la, la la, la, la…Isn't it romantic? Do, dodo, do, do do, do."

He laughs, stuffs the box in the car and starts singing his own tune. "Happy Birthday to you…I hope you like this woodsy present more than a new pair of shoes."

I wave a dried berry-filled branch at him. "Fine," I say, and pile in a few more sticks and other potpourri ingredients from the North Carolina countryside. "You know the best gifts are free. This tradition ushers in the holiday season for me. It's my way of taking a piece of the mountains home. And I can make lots of Christmas gifts with this stuff."

He brightens. "Does this mean you don't have to buy any Christmas gifts this year?"

At this point, I do my own eye-rollie thing and smile at him. "Only if you promise we can come back to the mountains for Christmas."

"What?" He backs away. "December 25 is not *your* birthday."

"You're right, I concede. We'll celebrate the most important birthday and have the merriest Christmas because of the priceless gift of love he freely gave."

We could agree on that.

My Favorite Christmas Potpourri Recipe

Mix:

>Pine cones, acorns, dried berries, small sticks, a few small river rocks

Add:

>Dried orange peels, sliced dried apples, cinnamon sticks, several drops of cinnamon oil

Gently toss all ingredients and arrange small mounds on large river rocks by the entrance of your home.

- Joann Claypoole

24

An Unexpected Christmas Gift

Guilt washed over me. We'd always put up our tree and other holiday decorations the Friday after Thanksgiving. Here it was the middle of December, and I'd not even pulled out the tree, or ornament and decoration boxes. I tried to muster up the enthusiasm and energy to get started, but my heart was still heavy because of limited funds reflected by the checkbook balance that morning.

I'd had excellent health until a few months before. Even though I'd seen several specialists, I still had no definitive diagnosis. The "within normal parameters" test results proclaimed by each doctor discouraged me. Would anyone ever diagnose my problem correctly?

It was becoming more difficult for me to continue my office job as I developed heightened sensitivities for second-hand smoke and fragrances, particularly perfume. My job performance became poorer and my absenteeism excessive. Finally, my boss and I decided I should resign.

With dwindling severance pay and no job offers, I became a temporary office worker. My counselor at the temp agency, considerate of my health challenges, assigned me to one-girl offices where I wouldn't encounter smokers.

Those job assignments typically lasted a week or two. At first I thrived on the challenge of getting used to the new boss, procedures, and equipment which came with each one, but the fascination quickly waned. My heart longed for the stability of a real job and identity within a permanent office setting. Being referred to as "the temp" annoyed me more and more.

At the beginning of December, I'd had an ear and throat infection, causing me to miss several days of work. With the slower holiday mail delivery, I realized my smaller paycheck wouldn't arrive in time to pay my health insurance. My morning's glimpse at my checkbook balance had confirmed that. Since I couldn't let the insurance lapse, I did what came naturally — I prayed. "Lord, please provide the needed money."

Feeling better and knowing that he was in control, I mustered up a little energy to pull out the tabletop Christmas tree. After setting it up, I began to wind the lights around the branches. Then the doorbell rang.

Annoyed because I didn't want to lose my momentum, I peeked through the window. John and Frank, two church deacons, stood on the front porch.

How odd. I'd never had a visit from the deacons, and I couldn't imagine why they'd come to visit me. I opened the door, smiled, and invited them in.

They sat down across from me, obviously uncomfortable. On the edge of their chairs, they fidgeted, played with their gloves, and looked at the floor.

Their nervous expressions and actions didn't encourage me. What was going on? Had I done something wrong?

After what seemed an interminable silence, John asked, "Any job prospects?"

"No, I'm still looking," I responded glumly.

By then, John worked up courage to plunge ahead. "As a member of the church, Joyce, you know about the deacon's fund, don't you?"

I nodded, and he continued. "The deacons met with the pastor this morning to pray about who the recipient of the fund should be this year. The Lord brought your name to each of us."

He then withdrew an envelope from his pocket and leaned to hand it to me. They seemed surprised when I took it, set it on my lap, and thanked them.

As I shared the story of my morning prayer, they relaxed, leaned back in the chairs and crossed their legs, but their eyes revealed astonishment. They smiled at each other and then back at me as they realized the envelope containing the church check was the answer to that prayer.

Frank then shared that he and John discussed my possible reaction on their way to my house. They expected me to be insulted and not accept it, embarrassing each of us.

They arrived in front of my house before they could formulate Plan B — what they would do if I didn't take it.

I laughed. "Now I understand why you were so nervous."

Sheepishly looking at each other and back at me, they joined in my laughter.

Frank prayed, thanking God for his provision and asking for a full-time job for me. Soon after, they hurried to their car, anxious to drive to church to share with our pastor the unexpected result of their visit.

After they left, I ripped the envelope open to peek at the check. The amount overwhelmed me. It not only covered my insurance bill and all the gifts on my shopping list, but a turkey dinner with all the trimmings. Even then, there would be some left over.

My heart thanked God for answering my prayer...beyond my expectation.

- Joyce Heiser

❧ 25 ☙
Gwen's Silent Night

Gwen brushed the snow from her collar and entered the nave, eyes downcast. A warm wave of scent, evergreen and candlewax, rushed around her tardy family of four, their only greeting. Gwen slid into the back pew after her husband, slipped the baby from her hip and unzipped his snowsuit in one fluid motion. She settled him on her lap and ran a shaking hand over the hat-loosened braids of her daughter.

She had not wanted to attend this service, her raw emotions a dangerous ground to tread, tonight of all nights, on Christmas Eve. But her husband had prevailed, and here they sat in a local church, the comfort of anonymity her single consolation.

The church looked like a Christmas card sprung to life, and her children were not alone in wide-eyed wonder as they took in the surroundings. Candlelight shone in the darkened space, its flickering touch of gold transforming ordinary objects into gilded vessels of worship. The pastor and choir in voluminous white robes were understudies for angels, completing mysterious, holy tasks behind the separating altar rail.

Gwen felt her emotions swell like a tide and sweep up the beach of her soul to mire her in the quicksand of barely-checked tears. She looked again to her children for some motherly distraction, any small chore to attend, but they required nothing from her.

The baby on her lap sat motionless, mesmerized by the play of light and the rising sound of the choir. Her daughter, standing between them, was on tiptoe, gazing across the aisle, scrutinizing the shadowy forms seated there.

So, with no barrier to slow them, Gwen's mother's words returned, scalding hot. "We will not be seeing you this Christmas, Gwen, or any Christmas. It is your fault that your children do not have the love of their grandparents. Consider this the consequence of your sins and do not call us again."

The words of her last conversation with her mother formed a condemning refrain: *Your fault. Your sins. Do not call us again.*

But she had called, again and again, passing the holiday months of November and December trying to bridge the gap, not only for herself, but also for the sake of her little family. Each time her finger circled the telephone dial, tracing the numeric address of her childhood in softly clicking loops, she was ready with a new plea or a fresh explanation. Not once had her mother picked up the receiver, no matter that she let it ring long, tense minutes until automatic disconnection.

The pastor's deep voice broke Gwen's dark thoughts and returned her with a jolt to her spot in the back row. He called the congregation to stand and take up candles tucked in advance among worn hymnals and bent envelopes. "Come, let us rejoice! The Light has entered the world! No longer do we sit in the darkness, a people without hope."

At this cue, the choir members offered their lit candles to the front row of congregants and the first verse of "Silent Night" floated upward, light as a feather. With careful contemplation, shaking wicks met in mid-air as tiny flames passed from one solemn participant to the next and spread backward through the crowd. The warm glow made its slow but steady advance on vast shadowy recesses, swelling in tandem with the traditional holiday anthem.

Silent Night, Holy Night…

The angry silence of her parents ground down upon her, and Gwen clutched her cold candle as weary tears traced hot paths down her cheeks. She pressed her face into the soft fragrance of her sleeping baby's neck and let hopelessness have its way. *Silent Night, indeed.* How long would her parents maintain their condemning silence, inflicting vengeance, even upon their own grandchildren? Would they never forgive her mistakes?

Her husband's warm hand on her back slowed Gwen's muffled tears. Their daughter perched on one arm, and with the other, he drew her to his side, into the security of his solid embrace.

Son of God, love's pure light…

Her daughter's tiny hand reached out to pat her hair with awkward motions.

Jesus, Lord at thy birth…

This small family, this wellspring of love and warmth, would have to be enough for her. Gwen knew it could be enough, if she could let the other go.

Shepherds quake at the sight…

Gwen lifted her face and gazed into her husband's brown eyes. She pressed a kiss into her daughter's hand and shifted the sleeping form of her son against her chest. At long last, Christmas light, carried by dime-store candles, reached the back row.

Glories stream from heaven above…

Gwen and her husband extended their candles at the same time, his hand firm with confidence and strength, her hand steadied with fresh hope.

Christ the savior is born, Christ the savior is born.

~ Susan Holt Simpson

❧ 26 ❧
The Christmas Tree Brooch

It's just a Christmas tree brooch. Metal, painted green, with little rhinestones glued in prongs on its small branches. Some might consider it an antique. After all, I've had it since I was ten, and I'm forty-six now.

I think after I die, the person going through my belongings will deem it worthless. They'll note that some of the rhinestones have fallen out and the paint has faded from the edges. As they toss it in the garbage, they'll probably wonder why in the world I held onto the thing. Their fashion sense might even be offended if they were to discover that I've worn it every Christmas season since it was given to me.

Lovey Sikes — Miss Lovey as we called her — was one of the old ladies in my church. Some of you remember those sweet, little women. Any child who overheard their conversations would believe that the only bright spot in the weekly drudgery of their widowhood was the preparation for, and attendance of, the Sunday morning church service.

Saturday existed solely for them to go to the beauty parlor, where their hair was washed and curled, teased and sprayed. And where the beautician always advised them to wrap their hair carefully that night in toilet paper, so sleep wouldn't damage their coiffure before the following morning's church service.

On Sunday morning, being proper Southern ladies, they donned girdles, support hose, their best dresses, low-heeled patent leathers, church hats and white gloves. Their purses weighed almost as much as they did, and were stocked with handfuls of butterscotch and peppermint candy.

Children flocked to them in the sanctuary aisles, around the pews in which they sat, and on the church steps where they stood visiting after the service.

Most of the kids clamored for the candy. But I sought the safe harbor those gentle spirits offered. The tenderness they bestowed was respite from the abuse that permeated my childhood.

Each time I pin the brooch to my lapel, I remember Miss Lovey and the day she handed me a small box, wrapped in pretty paper and topped with a bow. Inside, a tiny Christmas tree, metal, painted green, with colored rhinestone ornaments. And I'm reminded that I was loved when I was a child.

- Joni Vance

27

What a Gift!

We had stuffed ourselves with Mom's traditional Christmas breakfast. After the family cleared the table and gathered in the living room, Dad read the Christmas story from Luke 2 and prayed. We designated the youngest great-grandson, ten days shy of his third birthday, to help distribute gifts. Then Mom shared her request. "Wait a minute. Before we open gifts, I want us to do something new this Christmas. Let's go around the room and each person share something you're thankful for."

Although appropriate any time, Mom's suggestion was particularly meaningful in light of our family's recent history. Almost three years earlier, we had faced a grim prognosis for our young helper and his mother.

Because of severe respiratory distress, he had to be delivered via cesarean section seven weeks premature. Doctors remained guarded about his recovery. His mother's situation was far worse, with a diagnosis of severe cardiomyopathy. She was transferred to a hospital eighty miles from her baby. Doctors performed immediate surgery and placed her on an external heart pump.

My nephew signed for a possible heart transplant, if she survived. Miraculously, the baby went home in ten days. His mother, minus the heart pump and with her own heart, in a month. Both remain in good health.

My husband and I had spent the previous Christmas season in three different hospitals. A six-year survivor of a malignant brain tumor (a miracle story), he suffered a heart attack, probable stroke, severe brain injury from his fall, and a lack of oxygen when his heart and lungs ceased functioning. Following the emergency room consultation, family and friends prepared to say goodbye. However, when staff removed his respirator the following day, he breathed on his own and tracked motion and sound. The third day he sat alone and talked. While he still suffers some residual effects, his progress continues to astound his doctors…and us.

Our family had to delay that particular Christmas gathering until New Year's Eve, due to a funeral for Mom's sister, her last sibling, on Christmas

Eve. Although difficult in many ways, her service epitomized a celebration of life. Our aunt planned the entire service and insisted on quilts from her personal collection rather than flowers to adorn the casket and room. Through laughter and tears, we recalled our time together and looked forward to meeting again. The entire family later gathered at Mom and Dad's for a meal, memories, and music. Any time we get together, we sing.

With these events and more in all our minds, our offering of thanks rang especially true. And what better way to top it than with a sing-along led by our lovable little preschooler? His grandmother suggested "Away in a Manger," but he started instead with "Jesus Loves Me." Her request followed. And then his finale, "Happy Birthday" to Jesus.

Who needed presents with a day like that? Of course we tore into them, one at a time, with the little elf's enthusiastic help. What fun to watch him jump, clap, and laugh with delight when we opened each gift.

Remembering our family's near losses and the miracles of life that surrounded us made us humbly appreciate, as never before, the sacrifice God made on our behalf. He freely gave his precious Child to die for us. The miracle of Jesus' resurrection makes victory over sin and death available. God also wraps his children in a blanket of divine love, peace, joy, and comfort through every hardship.

What a gift!

- Diana Derringer

Thanks be to God for his indescribable gift!

2 Corinthians 9:15 NIV

❧ 28 ☙
Christmas Came

Christmas came for me
when I allowed Jesus
to outgrow swaddling clothes
and wrap me in God's love.

Christmas came for me
when I discovered that
I am part of the flock
God is watching over —
even at night.

Christmas came for me
when I rejoiced, knowing
Christ's tidings of great joy
were to all people —
and I'm a messenger.

Christmas came for me
when his love and wisdom
filled me to serve others
as my gold, frankincense
and myrrh.

~ Charlotte Adelsperger

29

Counting Southern Treasures Through the First Noel

Dearest Hayden Noelle,

It's nearing Christmas, the time the birth of Jesus Christ our Savior is celebrated, and I can't help but think about how blessed I am to have been brought up in the South — the Bible Belt, Chattanooga, Tennessee being the buckle of that belt — and to know the true meaning of Christmas.

As I'm driving through the gate that leads to your great-grandparents' retirement home on a mountain top in north Alabama, I remember the story Mother told of my niece and her first grandchild, Jessica, when they were in the car on their way to town. Before they left the mountain farm, the three-year-old jumped from the front seat to the back. Mother thought it strange that like lightning, she'd changed her seating arrangement. But then mother's nose began to twitch and she exclaimed, "Whew-eee! I think I smell a skunk!" The three-year-old held her perky nose and replied, "I know! I smell it too! And I think it's Paw Paw."

That is only one of the many funny family stories I recalled while driving down the road to the home place where so many Christmas celebrations were enjoyed after Meco and Paw Paw moved to their farm after leaving their city home.

Smoke now curls high above tall lonesome pines that stand around like soldiers guarding azaleas and roses that will once again bloom pink and white blossoms in spring. Opening the front door of the house with a stone foundation and a green tin roof, I'm now inside with memories flooding in through the foyer. I spot the cedar Christmas tree that always stood majestic in the corner so the lights could be seen through the window by visitors. The star on top shines, projecting a soft light to wayfaring strangers and friends alike. Lights bubble red, green, yellow, and blue, as cedar scent wafts through the cathedral-ceiling great room to mingle with the scent of pine boughs draped from a mantel graced with hoards of competing Santas of all shapes and sizes.

A crèche, complete with camels and wise men or magi bearing gold, frankincense, and myrrh, graces the antique Klondike ice box that once kept another of our log cabin's food cold with chunky blocks of ice but is now the keeper of crayons, coloring books, and secret little whispery girl things.

The smell of burning logs and hickory wood smoke emanates from the fire, one log tumbling from its high place and breaking in two before the mammoth back log, scattering red hot coals to the front of the deep hearth while sparks fly to be caught by the heavy fire screen guarding the yawning mouth of the cavernous fireplace.

Mother, or Meco as first grandchild Jessica dubbed her because she couldn't say grandmother, sits on her end of the sofa with excitement lilting her voice. She says, "Hear the tramping in the fireplace, girls? That means a snow is coming. It's time to string cranberries and popcorn for the tree. Who wants to help me make hot chocolate first?"

Down the hallway, I peek into the front bedroom where my toddler daughters slept — one of them is your Mama — when they weren't dreaming of visions of sugar plums dancing in their heads and fussing with each other over…well…just about everything. Mother's voice trills out of the master bedroom. "Paw Paw, go in there and tell your grandchildren to get quiet and go to sleep."

And Paw Paw replies, "Those are your grandchildren, Meco. You go tell them. Mine are in Memphis and that's where I hope they stay." And I could visualize his ears wiggling when he thought he'd made a funny. That's how I knew, when he had his back to me, if he was joking.

When I leave the hallway to step back down into the sunken family room, I hear Christmas packages being unwrapped, the tearing of tissue paper and the popping sound grosgrain ribbon makes when stretched tight to breaking, amidst Daddy's laughter right before he plops a chocolate covered cherry into his mouth and pipes, "Who is the prankster who gave me this rubber chicken?"

A smile covers my entire face and I stay silent, stepping up into the kitchen from the sunken family room. Daddy's one eyebrow raised as he stares suspiciously at me while Bing Crosby croons, "I'm dreaming of a white Christmas," from the ancient stereo's turntable.

It's in the kitchen's bay window where I hear the dessert table groaning from six or seven cakes — red velvet queen among them — and at least four meringue pies as the fried corn and okra stay warm while waiting on the turkey to fry. I count the other vegetable sides with cornbread dressing, broccoli and cheese casserole, and deviled eggs among many more long steaming Pyrex dishes of delights and wonder where the rolls will sit once heated and waiting to be drenched in butter before being washed down with sweet tea.

It's then Mother's voice calls from the family room. "Okay, now I've received two boxes of Chanel Number 5 bath powder. Maybe this will be another four-bottles-of-White-Shoulders-perfume Christmas like what happened one year when we lived in Chattanooga. Who knew I'd actually get what I hinted for this year!" And the fragrance of happiness and joy mingles with the nutmeg scent wafting from squares scored into a hunk of ham glistening from the oven that will feed over thirty hungry mouths.

Walking from the kitchen and into the mud room, I spy Great-Grandmother Shug's (Big Mama) old wood stove standing her ground in the corner, her new resting place once Big Mama had slipped through the veil to be with our Lord. And I can't count the many meals prepared on heavy stove eyes — not only in Big Mama's home but in the log cabin summer home on two hundred acres Meco and Paw Paw once owned at the foot of the mountain in an Alabama cove.

I remember sleeping in fluffy-fat feather beds one of my grandmothers had stitched, listening to mountain lions squall at night in the wooded thickets deep beyond chinked logs and screened windows that kept away the mosquitoes and bats, slithery crawlers and creatures, and icky-acky things that go bump in the night.

Stepping out onto the back porch to inhale fresh December air, I spot the hummingbird feeders and remember hoards of tiny ruby-throated birds flying in and treading air with their wings, waiting their summer turns while sipping from nearby Rose of Sharon tree blossoms. The trees are transplants from Grandmother's and Granddaddy's home place of nine hundred acres of farm and mountain land down the dirt road from our old farm that rested next to theirs.

I sit in Mother's rocker and rock, the cool breeze kissing my face.

And I rock some more, reminiscing about Daddy driving a tractor pulling a wagon of hay around the community to bring family and friends to our big bonfire wiener roasts that always guaranteed a marshmallow fight. Or two. Okay, maybe three to a dozen, when Meco and Paw Paw owned another farm in another sacred place.

It's from this very porch I can see down into the valley of autumnal cotton pickin' sunsets where Mother and Daddy and kindred spirits once trod. I also witness red tail hawks soaring and circling on wind drafts above the silver-ribbon Tennessee River. And from this porch rattlesnakes can sometimes be spotted snaking through tall grass along with rocky raccoon and a possum meandering through the back yard in search of discarded corn cobs and supper leftovers before they hole up somewhere to outlast the onslaught of winter.

I once even saw a red fox sneak through. He was headed for the ancient stone chimney near the spring that feeds the pond — all that's left of a great-uncle's home place that was settled early on atop this windswept rugged mountain where stars might be touched, if one only believes it can be done from a fairly tall ladder while standing on tippy-toes.

The soft lowing of a heifer breaks through my reverie, and I'm reminded of your Mother's on-the-spot song writing skills when Paw Paw was out of the truck feeding his cattle. I listen to a four-year-old daughter sing, "If the bully gets my grandfather, I'll run and save his life. I'll run and save his life." That talent must have come from her Scotch-Irish side along with those who originally hailed from England before sailing to Virginia to end up in Tennessee and North Alabama by way of North Carolina Revolutionary War land grants.

I leave the porch overlooking the valley below where my parents and ancestors are buried in a cemetery that overlooks a million footsteps that knew a ton of sorrow and wheelbarrows full of joy. I recall the many dinners on the ground next to the chapel Meco helped raise money to restore — now flattened by devastating tornadoes that uprooted coffins and gravestones alike while ripping ancient oaks from deep moorings to leave gaping holes in the ground.

But then I smile because a photo of Daddy and his kith and kin shows them eating dinner on the ground at the chapel, the inspiration for another beloved story. I think about you, the latest addition to our family, eight-months-in-the-womb Hayden Noelle — the first Noelle, or first birth-grandchild of mine belonging to your Mom's and Dad's next generation of new beginnings, new memories, and new Christmases.

I'll be back to rock some more on this mountaintop back porch while waiting to celebrate the birthday of our Lord. I overlook the paths of my ancestors who have already come and gone, while thinking about your arrival. I'm counting my Southern treasures as the guardian angels watch over us and rejoice at your coming. I can't wait to meet you, precious one.

And I can't wait to share with you about the very *first* Noel and the true meaning of Christmas. No matter how many homes and holidays and kith and kin come and go like the tides of the ocean rushing in to rush back out again, you will always have a Savior's birthday to celebrate, a Savior who is steadfast and true. For Jesus says, *"Be sure of this: I am with you always, even to the end of the age."* (Matthew 28:20b NLT)

With Love,

Lovie

For Your Very First Christmas.

~ Vicki H. Moss

～ 30 ～
A Pure and Simple King

My cousin, a Hollywood camera operator, showed me around the studio set of the latest television show he was working on. The show was a popular sit-com, and the two leading actors were household names. He took my picture as I sat in the pretend kitchen, and we wandered around the adjoining sets: a bedroom, a café, a school hallway. While I enjoyed the tour, I kept wondering to myself: How are they able to make any of this look even half-way real when the show airs on television? The sets seen up close were so flimsy and fake. To accept them as believable was giving in to an illusion.

But isn't that what Hollywood is, masterful illusion? More, isn't that how the world is, offering up its glamorous lies of wealth, power, and success as the "real deal," when these things have no genuine substance to satisfy our souls?

I love how Jesus, when it was time for him to come into the world, was born not in a palace, but in a barn. I love how he made of himself an ordinary person who lived in a small town and worked as a carpenter. And how, when he wandered from place to place during his years of ministry, he had no place to lay his head, which means he may very well have spent many nights sleeping on the ground under the stars.

Jesus came into the world to save us from death, but at the same time, he showed us how to live. His goal was to do the will of God, to complete the tasks God had sent him into the world to do. That's all. And for Jesus, that was enough. He never sought after power or wealth, or popularity, because he knew these things were only an illusion, a cheap imitation of what God wants to give us when we're in right relationship with him.

My favorite Christmas decoration is my Nativity scene, with baby Jesus lying in the manger. God himself, wrapped in swaddling clothes and sleeping on the hay. It reminds me of what brings true joy in this world: humbleness, servanthood, self-sacrifice.

The world's offerings of happiness are illusions. As tempting as they are to believe and pursue, choose instead to follow in the footsteps of the Christ child, a pure and simple king.

~ Ann Tatlock

❧ 31 ☙
Plan a Silent Night

Each December, my husband and I set aside one evening to listen to a recording of Handel's magnificent *Messiah*. The twinkling tree lights, blazing fire, and cups of hot chocolate create a cozy atmosphere as we listen to the music and focus on Jesus' birth. Sometimes my husband and I sing along. Other times we read Scriptures from which the lyrics are taken.

The words in Handel's *Messiah* come from both the Old and New Testaments. Since the melody often reflects the lyrics, the music paints a picture of the story. For example, Isaiah's words, "The people that walked in darkness," are sung in a slow, sad, minor key. As the bass soloist sings this aria, his notes move up and down the scale to reflect the wandering of the people, and the mournful melody conveys the sorrow and hopelessness of life without Jesus the Messiah.

But when the wonderful words from Isaiah 9:6 burst forth, "For unto us a child is born, unto us a son is given," the minor key changes to major and the somber sounds are replaced with joyous, lilting music. The tempo increases, and the music portrays the good news of Jesus' birth.

The choir continues, singing the names of Jesus, "Wonderful, Counsellor, the mighty God, the everlasting Father, the Prince of Peace." Each staccato phrase is emphasized, and the words and music convey a strong sense of authority, victory, and hope.

As I listen to the words and music, my heart dances. And when the triumphant "Hallelujah" chorus is sung, I stand in awe and worship of the King of kings and Lord of lords. The chorus ends with the jubilant words, "And he shall reign forever and ever. Hallelujah."

After an evening of listening to *Messiah*, I feel renewed physically and spiritually.

Perhaps you also would enjoy a slower pace during this busy season to reflect on the true meaning of Christmas. If so, you could bundle up on a starry night and take a walk around your neighborhood, imagining the wonder and surprise the shepherds felt when the angel chorus announced the good news of Jesus' birth.

Or as you walk, perhaps you'll ponder the journey of the wise men as they followed the star. Enjoy the holy hush of the evening and consider softly singing "Silent Night" together as you walk home. Afterwards, you could warm up by sipping steaming cups of hot chocolate with candy-cane stirrers, as you relax by candlelight.

If you have young children or grandchildren, consider surprising them with a pajama-clad car ride through the neighborhood to admire the Christmas lights. The discussion could center on how Jesus came to bring light to our dark world. Perhaps you'll sing Christmas carols as you travel, or listen to a recording of carols including "Silent Night."

Maybe, like my husband and me, you'll choose to listen to *Messiah*. Whatever your plans, take time to reflect on the true Gift, and rejoice that God's great gift of a child was given to us at Christmas. And that makes all the difference year-round and for eternity.

~ Lydia E. Harris

✥ 32 ✤
Provision in a Time of Need

A few years ago, within the span of a few months' time I had been laid off from my job, required multiple extensive vehicle repairs on both of our family's cars, faced the untimely demise of a few essential house appliances, experienced concerning medical symptoms which necessitated many tests to in order to rule out terrifying possible diagnoses, and learned our insurance would not cover the cost of those tests.

Winter in the bitterly cold Northeast was soon to arrive, and we had a non-working furnace...and no propane with which to fuel that furnace (were it to be fixed) or to run the water heater or cook-stove.

We also had no firewood with which to heat the house via our wood-burning stove, because the large mound of wood we had planned to split and use that winter had been swept downstream when a beaver dam upstream had breached. The freak flash-flood tore through our yard, carrying every non-stationary object with it.

A flood like that had never happened before, according to the old-timers who stood by the road watching our firewood and other yard-based possessions bobbing away in the fast-moving water.

That year, even though it had never flooded before in the memories of the town's octogenarians, our yard flooded twice (of course). Some neighbors had generously replaced a portion of our unfortunately buoyant pile of rock maple, but before we had a chance to figure out how to afford to add to that pile, Hurricane Irene came with a vengeance, ripping the countryside apart as her torrential downpours caused formerly meek waterways to swell to gargantuan proportions.

Two months after the first flood, I sobbed as I watched the precious firewood which replaced part of the original stack being carried off by yet another freak flood.

Winter was coming. We had no firewood, no propane, and no working furnace. We had spent all of our emergency funds on necessary repairs, and had nothing left. There was still more that needed to be fixed.

I had not been able to obtain new employment.

My unemployment money was about to run out.

I was scared that we were going to lose everything.

The future looked bleak and hopeless.

There was no way that we would even be able to continue to pay our bills, unless a miracle happened.

I could not see how we would make it through the winter.

My husband prayed that God would provide for us in a miraculous way. He prayed that I would be comforted in knowing that God had never failed us before, and that he would not fail us at this dark time.

Unbeknown to me, he had also prayed that God would provide extra work for him so he could earn what was needed to provide for his family. Even though he faithfully worked at his regular full-time job, because there had been no overtime opportunities for well over five years he had always taken on extra, back-breaking jobs in order to provide for our children and me.

The next day, I saw a request for information about gratitude at Christmastime that could be incorporated into a newspaper article. With previous serendipitous provisions in my mind after praying with my husband the day before, I sat down at the computer and sent off a quick email to the journalist. I offered a few examples of how we had been provided for before, and stated I was choosing to look through eyes of gratitude this particular Christmas, even though our circumstances looked bleak. I sent the email off, and went to take care of some housework.

Five minutes later the phone rang. It was my husband. He said he had just gotten off the phone with an engineer who had contacted him to request his assistance with a project. This engineer had heard a lot about my husband's integrity and excellent work ethic and had decided he wanted my husband's regular help over the following months for this project. It meant he would receive over twenty hours of overtime each week.

Talk about a miracle — I bawled.

After the phone conversation with my husband, I went to my computer to check my email. To my surprise, there was already a reply from the newspaper reporter. He wanted more information from me. I sent him the data he wanted, and less than two minutes later, received another reply from him which stated that he wanted to write an article on what I had sent him about looking at gratitude in the midst of hardship during the Christmas season. I excitedly agreed, thinking it might encourage someone else to have hope in the midst of a hopeless-looking circumstance.

To my extreme embarrassment, the published article focused on my recent circumstances of losing a job, having many unfortunate events occur, and how my family and I were choosing to express gratitude in the middle of it all by developing innovative activities to celebrate the birth of Christ rather than dwelling on the lack of presents that year.

A few days later, I received an anonymous letter in the mail. The writer graciously expressed a compassionate heart for my family, and enclosed a money. The amount was enough to cover the purchase of propane for the water heater and cook-stove as well as the sorely-needed firewood.

Later the same day, some sweet people stopped by to give us gift cards. They wanted to express their gratefulness to my husband for serving his country as an infantryman in the Iraq war. The gift cards provided enough for us to purchase not only food to refill our empty cupboards and refrigerator, but also other household necessities which had run out that very day.

There was even enough left over to be able to purchase the one gift my son and daughter had wanted, but knowing we didn't have the extra money that year, did not ask for. Their faces on Christmas morning, when they received the present they had so very much wanted, brought me unspeakable joy.

That wasn't all. One neighbor *just happened* to stop by and ask if we could use a free set of tires for our car. He had bought a new car, and had an extra set for his older car lying around. He didn't know our car's tires were so bald it was unsafe to drive, or that it was the last day of the month in which that car was due for an inspection.

Another kind man took up a collection at work and gave us another gift card, which enabled me to purchase badly-needed clothing and shoes for the children.

The provisions did not stop.

Miraculously, we made it through that winter. The weather was mild enough for us to use only the wood-burning stoves, not the furnace, for heat. We had just enough wood and propane to last through the winter.

We were able to pay all of our bills and keep our house.

My medical tests came back negative.

When times get tough — and they do — I look back on that season of impossible obstacles, and take hope in knowing that "serendipitous" events do happen. We just have to be ready — and willing — to be a part of them.

God comes through, providing opportunities for us to seize and make the most of, as well as prompting people to take opportunities to bless us.

~ Marybeth Mitcham

33

Sunshine for Christmas

When I heard my younger sister's car pull into my parents' driveway, I hurried out to greet her. Sylvia was home from college for the Christmas holiday.

After giving her a hug, I went around to the passenger side window, anxious to see the chocolate and caramel-colored Chihuahua/terrier mix who'd ridden all the way from Sylvia's apartment in Virginia to my parents' home in Connecticut.

"Hi Sunshine," I said as I tapped on the window. "Did you enjoy the trip?"

Sunshine looked up at me with her dreamy eyes, stood on hind legs and smeared the window with her moist snout.

"Hi Sunshine!" my mother shouted as my sister carried the chubby dog into the house. Sunshine wheezed and squawked as mom and I petted her. With the dog's head drooped listlessly on her shoulder, Sylvia carried Sunshine up the stairs to her childhood bedroom.

"I do hope Sunshine enjoys her time here," my mother said. "I've got a special Christmas gift for her later today, after she settles in and gets some rest."

We wanted Sunshine to feel comfortable with us. On a previous visit, she'd barely left Sylvia's side. Sylvia had found the dog months earlier at her apartment complex. It was wearing a collar, but no tags. She'd put up flyers in the neighborhood looking for the owner, but no one had claimed her. Days later, when Sylvia had found the dog standing in a puddle near her front door after an overnight rainstorm, she decided to adopt her. She knew the dog would brighten her life, so she'd named her Sunshine.

Sylvia said they'd became instant buddies. On nice days she'd take the dog on strolls through the park. Sometimes they'd lie on the couch and watch soap operas together after Sylvia returned from class.

But when Sylvia had taken Sunshine for her first checkup, the veterinarian's findings troubled her. He'd said Sunshine was an old dog, probably between ten and twelve. The vet had diagnosed the dog as having a collapsed windpipe, which caused the squawking and wheezing, common among some toy breeds and terriers. The condition was not life threatening, but there was no known treatment for it. He'd advised Sylvia not to allow Sunshine to get excited.

In addition, Sunshine had a bad back, hearing loss, and cataracts, which gave her eyes a dreamy look. She also had fluid gathered around her heart. The vet had advised Sylvia to carry Sunshine up flights of stairs so she wouldn't overexert herself. He prescribed pills for the condition, which Sylvia had to slip down the dog's throat daily.

Later in the day they arrived, Sylvia wanted to go out to catch up with some former high school friends, so she brought Sunshine downstairs. As soon as my sister shut the front door behind her, the dog sat on her haunches facing it and refused to budge.

Eventually she slowly padded away looking dejected, head down, and ears flapping. She attempted to hobble up the stairs, but before she got past the first step, I took her in my arms and carefully carried her to my parents' bedroom.

Meanwhile, my mother went to the kitchen to bake cookies. My parents' godchildren, a three- and four-year-old brother and sister, would come over later. Mother would put the cookies under the tree so the children could see we were expecting Santa. The cookies would be crunchy oatmeal raisin, one of Santa's favorite kinds.

I gave Sunshine a back and shoulder rub. She didn't react at first but after a while she seemed to enjoy the attention. She licked my hand, and began to doze.

After the cookies had cooled, my mother put them on a tray and placed them under the Christmas tree for Santa. When Sylvia returned, Mother presented her with a box. "This is for Sunshine," she said. "See if she likes it."

Sylvia opened the box. Inside was a green and red sweater, just the right size for a pint-sized dog. The sweater was personalized with Sunshine's name embroidered across the chest in elegant script. Sunshine sat patiently as Sylvia pulled the sweater over the dog's head and squeezed her paws through the openings for the front legs. Mother went through her wrapping paper drawer and found a red bow. She attached it to Sunshine's collar.

After Sunshine was dressed, she didn't lie down and nap as we expected.

Soon, she was trotting around the house. She had pep in her step. She seemed to take pride in her Christmas sweater. When Sylvia put that sweater on her, Sunshine apparently sensed the love and care of the family that surrounded her.

Later that day, as we wrapped gifts and arranged them under the Christmas tree, we noticed that the cookies for Santa were missing. A few crumbs were left behind, but otherwise there was no trace of what had been there. We looked at Sunshine, who was licking her mouth.

Sylvia didn't scold her. She scooped her up in her arms and gave her a hug. Mother and I petted her. Sunshine wheezed and squawked. She'd worked up an appetite, found a hidden treasure, and was dressed in holiday finery that put us all in the Christmas spirit.

- Lisa Braxton

34

Christmas Caper

I may have inherited my mother's face, but my facial expressions and my wit are all Daddy's. I knew as soon as I stepped into my parents' delightfully decorated living room on Christmas Eve and saw the crooked little grin that turned up only the right side of his mouth and the sparkle of mischief in Daddy's cornflower-blue eyes, that someone was going to be the recipient of some tomfoolery he considered hilarious. How many times had I glanced in the mirror and seen that same look reflected back at me when I was up to no good?

I had traveled from Placerville, California to Klamath Falls, Oregon with my two children, Tina, eleven, and Kurtis, eight, to celebrate a Brown Family Christmas with my parents. Weather delayed us and we had spent the night waiting out blizzard-like conditions at a motel in Redding. We arrived safely after a slow, white-knuckle drive of one hundred forty miles with tire chains chattering over rutted snow-packed roads. We had passed numerous overturned cars in roadside ditches with colorful, wrapped packages tossed topsy-turvy, visible through upside down windows.

The familiar scents of Mother's Christmas baking wrapped around me like a warm comforting fleece when I stepped out of the car into the knee-deep snow. Mother and Daddy's home was a Christmas wonderland. Not a table top was left without angel or elf. Tributes to the religious significance of Christmas were prominent as were the secular. Ornaments that adorned the tree when I was a child again hung on the branches. Ceramic reindeer pranced across the mantel and candles shone from window sills. Dishes of homemade candies were within easy reach from every chair.

Even in the bathrooms, signs of Christmas were on the countertops and a felt-Santa modestly shielded his eyes with green-mittened hands on the underside of the toilet lid cover. I loved coming home for Christmas. It was important for me to bring my children to the nurturing arms of family tradition to celebrate the birth of Jesus — important enough to risk traveling in a winter storm.

I had adopted my children. Mother and Daddy loved them. Daddy, named Tom, who the children called "Tombo," especially enjoyed telling riddles and pulling pranks on Tina. She'd even bought a joke book with her allowance in an attempt to keep up with him.

On this Christmas Eve, I didn't know what Daddy was up to, but it was clear to me, at least one trick was hidden up his grandfatherly sleeve. He was antsy. He kept looking at his watch. His impish grin was stuck on his face. Like a little boy waiting for the arrival of the "right jolly old elf," Daddy could hardly contain himself. But, the Brown family had their customs and Mother cared about rituals, so Daddy's monkey-business, whatever it was, would have to wait.

While the kids busied themselves with package sleuth detail, Mother and I set the dining table for our Christmas Eve dinner, a more laid-back preview of the next day's feast. Mother was a great cook and hostess. She made it all look easy. Daddy sat in his recliner intermittently checking his watch and teasing the kids about their gifts. Even while we ate, the twinkle of naughtiness never left Daddy's eyes. I saw him exchange knowing looks with my mother who apparently was an accomplice in this hoax.

After dinner, our routine was to let the children open one gift. They were never surprised. The gifts were always a girlie Christmas nightgown for Tina and a pair of Christmas colored sweats for Kurtis to sleep in.

Mother and Daddy's house was a large split level with bedrooms on both floors. There were more than enough beds for everyone. But, Tina resisted change. Her choice for years was to sleep under her grandparent's antique Victorian-era bed with just her head sticking out from under the ornately carved walnut footboard. As soon as she was dressed in the new nightgown, she situated her sleeping bag under the bed, said her "good-nights" and slid herself into position.

With the kids in bed, I thought whatever Daddy was up to must be happening in the morning. When Daddy left the room, I didn't think anything of it. In just a few minutes however, I began to hear what sounded like the rattle of chains. From the darkened hallway, I could see the faint glow of colored lights. I hurried into the hall in time to see my six foot two inch, sixty-five-year-old father clad in a heavy orange winter hunter's jacket with the hood pulled over his head. He had wrapped himself in chains and multi-colored Christmas tree lights. With an extension cord, he plugged himself into a hallway socket. He walked carefully, stiff and mummy-like, into the bedroom he shared with Mother.

Mother and I arrived in the doorway in time to watch as he approached Tina's now sleeping head protruding from under the bed. The chains continued to clang together as Daddy bent down close to the relaxed youthful face and said in a slow deep voice peppered with laughter, "Ho, Ho, Ho, Tina. I am the Ghost of Christmas Past."

Tina aroused from her Christmas Eve slumber to a human light display just inches from her face. Was she scared? Well, maybe of the Ghost of Christmas Past, but not of her Tombo. For the rest of Daddy's life, the two of them laughed and reminisced about the best Christmas Eve stunt of all times.

Tina is forty years old now. Tombo's Ghost of Christmas Past escapade left us with cherished memories for Christmases — present and future. If I thought I could pull it off, I'd cast myself in Daddy's role and revive the scene for my grandchildren. I think it is just best, however, if every year on Christmas Eve we sit around the tree, tell the story and let young imaginations add their own sparkle and plot their own Christmas capers.

- Karen R. Hessen

❧ 35 ❧
When God Heals a Christmas Memory

"Choose something you want," my mother quietly said as we ambled our way up and down the aisle of our local department store. With Christmas only a handful of days away, my choices were limited. Christmas paper, bows, and ribbons were stamped with evidence of those trying to dig through what was left during the Christmas rush. Misfit toys spilled from torn packages. None of them cradled the baby doll I had hoped to see that Christmas morning, but I had to choose something.

I don't remember the face of the doll I chose that cold December night but the sadness in my mother's face would never be forgotten. As an eight-year-old child, I didn't understand how anyone could look so unhappy during a time that was supposed to be the happiest time of the year. However, later on I learned it was anything but happy for my mom — and for good reason.

On the day after Thanksgiving, my dad decided to leave in search of a new life — one that didn't include Mom. He was the only man she'd ever loved, sweethearts since the seventh grade. She wasn't emotionally prepared for the news and it left her numb, and raw with sorrow. Looking back, I realize she was simply in survival mode, going through the emotions. Her security blanket now offered no security at all.

My first Christmas memory from that night in the department store began to emerge when I faced my own first Christmas as a single mom many years later. The difference is that I was the one who left in search of a new life. Being divorced twice by the age of twenty-seven left me feeling like a misfit toy spilling out of its comfortable box, on display for all to see. Shame followed me wherever I went. It was then, however, that God drew me to him. He slowly began healing the eight-year-old within, wrapping my wounds with his grace.

Like my mom all those years ago, I too struggled financially but that year was different. God changed my focus. I was fixated on the true Gift-giver rather than the material gifts I could or could not provide for my boys. On Christmas Eve, after I'd tucked them into bed, I sat beside our Charlie Brown-look-alike tree and began writing on separate pieces of paper the gifts God had given me and my family of three in recent months: priceless peace, grace, mercy, freedom from shame, his strength and truth. As tears of thankfulness fell, I neatly folded each piece of paper, placed a bow on top, and put them beneath our tree. Those were the only gifts I opened that Christmas morning — and they were the only ones I needed.

With each bow that hit the floor that morning, I sensed the sadness from my first Christmas memory melting away, ushering in a kind of joyfulness I'd never known. It was an unexpected gift, the kind of gift that isn't delivered on a bright red sleigh once a year, but rather, from the hand of One who can heal all hearts, making the true spirit of Christmas available every single day.

~ *Cathy Baker*

❧ 36 ❧
Jesus in a Barn

Christmas is my favorite time of year, a season associated in my mind with decorated trees, candlelight services, cozy fireplaces, and the warmth of family, friends, and lots of good comfort food.

That year, however, was my first as a missionary in South Asia, where the season meant elephants were coming down from the jungle into the outlying villages foraging for food, and the warmth came from sweating under six yards of sari material in the tropical heat.

Instead of a comfortable, cushioned pew at church, I sat outside that Christmas morning in a chair that rocked back and forth on the uneven ground (not to be confused with a rocking chair). The women were on one side, the men on the other, and of course neither the singing nor the sermon were in English. We were a rainbow, at least the women's side, our saris in every color imaginable, each flowing out behind us as we sat with our legs curved to the side to avoid our feet facing anyone and thus insulting them.

It was certainly no white Christmas — most of the people around me had never seen snow except in the Americans' photographs.

Up front, the stage was decorated with the bright, lavishly colored cloths that signify celebration. Blue and green cloths draped across the top, while pink cloths bearing sketches of palm trees, hills, and birds bordered the sides.

After the service came visiting time, which is how they celebrate Christmas day. We left the patchwork places and wandered from one mud house to another. The missionaries were repeatedly stuffed with various local sweets and tea at each house, our hosts saying, "If you love us, you will eat more."

The most memorable part of that Christmas season came from a group of children, the missionary kids, who had invited us to see a nativity drama they had prepared. We followed the children down the brick path toward a very small authentic local barn, complete with authentic smells. It was big enough for the few children acting, a cow, several small, noisy animals, and us uncomfortable spectators. It was hot and musty and dark.

The clucking chickens and the lowing cow were quite distracting. I had never thought of that all those years when I sang, "The cattle are lowing," from the song "Away In a Manger."

I wanted to be sitting in an air-conditioned church, watching a clean, music-filled presentation of this wondrous event.

As I stood there, sweating and wishing I could leave, the children told the old, old story of Mary and Joseph and a baby. In a barn. A real barn, complete with animals and authentic smells. A real couple, who had just traveled a long and difficult journey, who had probably not had a bath since they arrived. A woman who delivered a baby into this raw arena, and who laid Him to rest in a feeding trough stuffed with hay — not because it sounded like a quaint idea for future tree ornaments, but because there was no bed for her baby.

It wasn't the comfortable, clean, well-packaged scene I'd seen reenacted time and again. It was raw life. Real life. God leaving all the glories of heaven to come and dwell among us in the lowliest, humblest, smelliest circumstances.

That day I realized that what made it wondrous was not how comfortable it was, how heavenly it felt. Just the opposite. It was how real and everyday and earthly it was.

That was the point.

John 1:14 tells us *the Word was made flesh and dwelt among us, and we beheld His glory.* (NKJV)

That Christmas, I had the gift of celebrating without the help of a Christian culture, without all the extras we add to help us feel more Christmassy. I was reminded in a beautiful way, as children proclaimed, "Behold, I bring you good tidings of great joy!" that God became flesh and dwelt among us — not in the King's palace with fanfare or even a comfortable church, but in a lowly place, one where the most humble, dirty, sweaty shepherd would feel at home.

Finding Jesus in a hot, smelly, noise-filled barn — what a novel thought.

~ Kimberly Rae

❧ 37 ❦
Favored by His Death

I rarely fail to cry when I hear "Silent Night, Holy Night." Perhaps because as a mother, I relate to this quiet moment of peace Mary was able to take in as she rocked her infant son.

It's that moment after birth, when a mother's eyes meet her child's for the first time — when the magic of motherhood physically flows from her, covering her infant. It's an instance of silence, when the heart of a mother speaks mentally to her child and a bond is formed — one that is rarely ever broken.

Mary was favored by God to bring his son into the world. His words brought her joy, but also unrest. Even with the assurance of this child's plight, she was blessed. And Mary recognized that.

I can't imagine her agony as she sat at the foot of the cross, his blood pooling at her knees. I can't begin to fathom the pain she suffered being so close, and still unable to comfort him or prevent the events that would kill him.

Even through her pain, Mary was favored and she recognized that.

My child, my gift from God, was less than perfect by the world's standards. His abilities limited, his path set, I could do little to cushion the blows of life. As a new mom, I was favored as well, blessed to have this baby. But what hovered over me were the things I would not be able to change or prevent that would try to rob me of the joy.

Despite the hardships, I have never felt anything less than favored and blessed, just as I know Mary must have felt.

Still, when our Christmas tree flickers in the darkened house, my heart breaks for the mother of Jesus. When the tiny Christmas music box on the piano tings out "Silent Night," I find myself sobbing inconsolably for a mother who lost her son because…of…me.

And yet, she is favored above all others and blessed even in her loss. Her child's destiny was Savior of the world, sent with the specific purpose to save our souls.

Silent night. Holy night. When all was calm. When all was bright. A holy infant slept in peace — heavenly peace.

Before you close your eyes on Christmas night, hum this tender song and ask for forgiveness so His death was not in vain. Mary was favored to bring this Christ child into the world, but you are favored by his death.

- Cindy Sproles

❧ 38 ❧
Steeped in Christmas Tradition

I held my favorite teapot in both hands, feeling its warmth and savoring the scent of the cinnamon as the tea steeped. The recent conversation with my husband was, however, neither warm nor savored.

"It's not about the money," he'd assured me last night while I turned pages in Christmas catalogs, searching for ideas. "It's about priority. The priority shouldn't be getting the best gift, or the latest technology, or trying to spend the same amount on each gift. It should be a focus on Christ. Besides, the grandkids already have more toys than they play with."

Gary and I had gotten into our annual discussion about gift giving. While we totally agree that society's emphasis becomes more secular each year, we differ on how to deal with it in our family.

He's a generous man who dislikes shopping and waiting in line, and hasn't a materialistic bone in his body. He would be content to neither give nor receive gifts.

On the other hand, I enjoy shopping and choosing gifts for those I care about — and I confess I also enjoy receiving…especially things that say, "You matter to me."

Not all gifts are wrapped or under the tree. Time with our grandsons, reading Christmas stories, drinking hot chocolate, or watching Christmas movies is something I treasure.

For several years, I hosted two separate Grandma's Craft Time weekends. The result was handmade gifts, from the boys, for the rest of the family. The experience was a gift I looked forward to giving, one I hope will continue to teach them the blessing of giving of themselves. Their excitement on Christmas Day, as they gave their gifts, was a blessing to me.

Unlike Gary, I'm not ready to stop shopping for Christmas presents. "I enjoy giving gifts," I said to the teapot, filling my cup. "I especially enjoyed it when all the kids were little," I added, remembering the fun of buying preschool toys and clothes.

I spooned honey into the tea and stirred. Hmm. The situation had actually evolved into a workable solution. I searched catalogs, narrowing possibilities. We decided together. I placed orders or shopped. We did usually shop together once, enjoying lunch out. Gary also does the wrapping, as that's definitely not one of my gifts.

Admittedly, adult children, spouses and seven grandsons have increased our Christmas spending. *Am I wrong?* Is giving gifts too important to me? Am I trying to impress them or buy their love?

"No," I said aloud. "I don't go over budget and I don't choose a gift just because it will be seen as expensive or the latest thing."

As I watched the honey dissolve in the small whirlpool, the kitchen of my childhood home eased itself into my mind. I was eleven years old. Cold December air came through the door with my dad. I could almost feel its chill. He stood straight and tall. His dark brown hair had a consistent wave that has been passed through at least four generations. With laughing eyes, he pulled a bank envelope from inside his jacket.

He grinned and handed it to me. "This is for you."

Fifty dollars! I'd never seen a fifty-dollar bill before.

"Wow! Is this really mine?" I asked. "How come?"

"Thought you might want to do a little Christmas shopping," he said.

My parents had always budgeted. Christmas was no exception. Each January they opened a Christmas Club account — a special savings account offered by most banks long before the bankcards of today. Several amounts were offered, with deposits made weekly. At the end of fifty weeks, the customer received the amount saved. They had opened one for me into which Daddy had paid one dollar a week.

"I see you have your surprise," Mother said, coming into the room.

"It's fifty dollars!" I showed her the money. "Daddy said it's for Christmas shopping! I've never given people presents just from me."

"We think you're old enough to do just that," she said.

"I've gotta go make my list! When can I go shopping?" I tore out of the room. From the hall, I stopped and turned. "Thank you."

When the weekend arrived, Mother and I went to Covington to shop.

Going through the doors of the department store, Mother asked, "Who's on your list?"

"Daddy first," I answered. "Then I've got Grandma and Aunt Mary, Aunt Nina, and…" I named grandparents, aunts, uncles, and probably cousins. I'd asked Daddy to take me shopping for Mother's gift so she wouldn't see what I bought for her.

"Then we'll go to the men's department first. What would you like to get for Daddy?"

When I saw the table filled with flannel shirts of all colors and patterns, I knew this was the right spot. I chose a blue plaid one. "Do you think he'd like this?" I asked, a little uncertain. It was for Daddy, and had to be just right.

"Perfect," she answered. "You know he wears them a lot, and he looks really good in blue."

By the time we left the department, I'd chosen flannel shirts for all my uncles and my grandfather, as well. I couldn't wait to wrap all my gifts.

Returning my thoughts to the present, I poured another cup of tea, remembering the assortment of potholders and handkerchiefs for the women on my list. In my head was the sound of paper rustling when I carefully wrapped each gift and proudly wrote names on the gift tags.

"Now I understand," I said aloud. "*That's* why I enjoy giving gifts!"

With that first Christmas Club account, my parents taught me much more than simply giving Christmas gifts. I remember the surprised and pleased responses as family members opened their gifts — and the joy I felt in giving. They taught me that giving is as much fun as receiving, if not more. Decades later, I still feel that child-like joy in giving to people I love.

And Gary…although we have our Christmas discussions about shopping or not, he still wraps the presents for me. And even wears a smile on his face.

~ Victoria Hicks

39

Make Peace with the Past

It was Christmas morning 1997. Wrapped in my light blue robe dotted with teddy bears, I sat curled up in the corner of the couch. The darkness of the wee morning hours engulfed the room. With coffee mug in hand, I stared at the Christmas tree. Its lights glistened through the tears filling my eyes and cascading down my cheeks. Sadness enveloped me as I remembered past Christmases and pondered what new ones would bring. I didn't know what the future held, but I was sure of one thing. This would be our last Christmas spent together as a family. Within a couple of months, the divorce would be final.

As I look back, that morning is still a blur. I don't remember much except the awkwardness of exchanging gifts for the last time with the man I had married almost twenty years earlier. As I think about it now, I can't imagine what thoughts and anxieties ran through the minds of our three sons. Were they scared? Were they sad like me? Despite the joy we tried to share, it was a hard morning for all of us.

Yet, over time and through the grace of God, I learned to forgive. I knew that I did not want to live harboring hatred in my heart. In order to move past the darkness that resided in my soul, I had to face a lot of things about myself, my relationships, and my attitudes.

With a heart-wrenching cry to God one night, down on my knees beside my bed, I relinquished the unforgiveness I harbored. When God took it from me, he filled me with his peace. I knew immediately that even though I would never forget, I could live life peacefully with the father of our boys.

From that point on, I made an effort to love my ex-husband despite what we had been through. I decided for the sake of our children, my extended family, and myself that reconciliation was what God was asking of me. When I made an effort to put the past behind me and move forward with love and forgiveness, wounds began to heal. Slowly, over time, the deep throbbing pain subsided.

Although some scars from the past still remain, they are present reminders of the future. They remind me that God reigns sovereign over my life. If I look to him for direction, he will guide me. If I look to him for comfort, he will comfort me. If I trust him, he will not let me down. I have learned that in his time, he will make all things new.

Years later, my ex-husband and I were in attendance for our grandson's preschool Christmas program. Together, even though our lives are much different, we shared the joy of watching the little one sing. Our lives have continued to stay connected, and God has blessed our families despite the initial pain we experienced not so many years ago.

My prayer today is one of forgiveness. Forgive the past. Move forward in love. And when you do, God's love will bring wholeness, happiness and peace.

~ Sheryl Baker

๑ 40 ๖

How Could I Manage Without It?

There was nothing special about the spoon. It was long-handled metal with a rubber end to protect the hand. But it was the only cooking spoon I had. It was Christmastime in 1987 and my husband had not been able to find a job for over a year. While preparing our dinner one evening, the rubber end broke off the spoon, rendering it useless. I didn't have any money to buy a new one. I didn't have any money to buy Christmas gifts for the children. All my pent-up emotion of our circumstances poured out the moment the spoon broke.

I felt broken, just like the spoon. That utensil represented everything that had gone wrong in the past couple years after we lost our business. My husband heard my sobs and came into the kitchen. He saw the broken spoon in my hand.

Gently, he removed the spoon and laid it on the counter. He took me in his arms and held me. No words were exchanged. There was no need.

The next day was Christmas, and it was snowing. Perfect. We lived in a remote area surrounded by acres of woods. The beauty of the forest was breathtaking. What fun we would have playing in the snow with our children! The freshness of the pure white snow seemed to send the message that this New Year would be a new beginning. I found solace in that.

We had some small gifts for the children under the Christmas tree and they had used their imagination to make us each a small token of love. Then I saw it.

On the kitchen counter was my spoon. My favorite spoon. I couldn't believe my eyes. It had a new wooden handle. I had no idea where he got it or how he did it, but my husband had found a piece of wood to fit the spoon. My spoon. It could still be used. I got so excited I believe the children were concerned that Mom had lost her faculties.

However, the lesson they learned that day was priceless. They understood the joy that comes when giving a gift from the heart.

All of us have had experiences like this that make us realize what is important. What love is.

That happened almost thirty years ago and I am still using the spoon. Every…single…day.

Every day I am reminded to find a way to make a gesture, no matter how small, to show appreciation to those I love. We may never know the impact it could make. I will never forget it.

~ Carol Graham

41
The Warmth of Christmas

As I bundled up my daughter for a cold evening of hopping in and out of the church van to carol at the local nursing homes, I began to wonder if all the activity was really worth the misery. It was the middle of December, and for all my scrambling around, I still hadn't managed to get everything done.

Every page of my planner was completely full of one thing or another, and I could think of much more practical ways to spend that Monday evening. Life as a single mom was hard enough — considering my full-time job, demanding housework, and daily motherhood requirements like returning the now-three-days-late cartoon videos, bandaging the occasional boo-boo, and reading the kindergarten progress reports.

Then, Christmas was thrown into the mix, with its parties and gift exchanges and shopping lists and baking and school plays and choir concerts. December had quickly become an unconquerable scheduling and financial monster.

Could I really spare this one Monday evening for Christmas caroling? Besides, why should I?

I didn't personally know any of the people we were visiting, and I certainly could not carry a tune. Of course, as she had done many times before, my very wise little girl quickly tapped my conscience ever so abruptly on its cold shoulder. As I zipped up her favorite pink coat, tucked in her striped scarf, and tied her toboggan straps around her chin, she said, "Let's give them some smiles, Mommy."

Ouch.

The Bible reminds us frequently that our own tongue can prove to be our enemy. How true this is! Just days before, when I was trying to figure out the best way to explain to my daughter why she simply couldn't buy fifty presents for every person she knew, I had said to her, "Honey, the best gift you can give anybody is a hug and a smile."

Why in the world did I go and tell her something like that?

At the time, I had said it in desperation, but I had no idea she'd remember it long enough for it to come back and bite me.

In my heart, I was far from practicing what I was preaching. I was demanding one thing from my child and not demanding the same thing from myself.

Ezekiel recognized this harsh reality well: *"My people...sit before you to listen to your words, but they do not put them into practice. With their mouths, they express devotion, but their hearts are greedy..."* (Ezekiel 33:31 NIV). Things really haven't changed much since the biblical days.

The inevitable burden of Christmas wish lists and constant gift exchanges have a way of wreaking havoc on the bank account and sanity. When trying to stretch a single secretary's income to heat the house, keep the lights on, put gas in the car, and keep groceries in the fridge, the holidays can be downright frightening.

The hugs-and-smiles routine helps ease the guilt of the empty checkbook and barren Christmas tree, but it's really not simply a routine at all. It is a truth about giving that we all should be teaching our children while learning it for ourselves: We should never become "weary in well doing." From the widow's mite to the story of the Good Samaritan, God commands us to be kind and to give not only of our material possessions but also of our time and of ourselves.

On that cold Monday night, my little girl reminded me of that important truth. As we walked down the halls and through the lobbies of the nursing homes and the residents were greeted with our singing and the smiles and embraces of my daughter and the other children in our group, I learned a great deal about Christmas.

I learned that when I don't have the resources to give from the mall, I can give something much more valuable that comes from the heart. This is a lesson we can all afford to learn and one we should be teaching our children.

Praise God I learned that no matter what we have or don't have, we can always give or share something — even if it is just a couple hours of time or a few smiles and hugs to a lonely person on a cold December night.

- Autumn J. Conley

❧ 42 ☙
The Last Doll

Every fall when the store shelves fill up with toys, my mind goes back to one of my favorite Christmas memories — the year I got a gift I dreaded receiving. Why would I cherish a memory about a present I didn't want in the first place? Well, to understand that, you have to believe the old adage, "It's the thought that counts."

Like most little girls, I loved dolls. I never owned the kind of dolls many girls get today — painted porcelain beauties lavishly dressed to put on a display stand, or authentically dressed dolls representing a specific period in American history and calling for accessories that cost as much as furnishing a small apartment.

I had dolls that were made for cuddling, not collecting.

My Tiny Tears doll drank a bottle of water and wet, but that was it. Today's dolls walk, giggle, sing, burp, and carry on more complex conversations than some husbands. I can still remember the thrill of getting a Thumbelina whose head moved around in slow circles after I wound the large button sticking out of her back. Of course, in order to see her move, I had to sit very still and concentrate.

Today we can shop for dolls that crawl, dance, or even do gymnastics. In the old days, dolls had just enough realism to make them exciting to a child, but not enough to crowd out imagination.

Living in the country with three brothers who mostly played war games, I treated my dolls like best friends. Dragging them all over the farm and into the woods meant they received a lot of wear and tear along with the love. And since one of my brothers got a kick out of ripping off their soft rubbery fingers and toes, I pretty much had to get a new doll every year.

In the world of the fifties and early sixties, I felt no pressure to grow up and leave childish things behind. I'm sure I clung to tree climbing and grapevine swinging longer than most of my friends. But by the seventh grade I was reading teen magazines and had traded in my Sunday socks for nylon hose. When Christmas drew near, for the first time ever, my wish list did not include toys. So when my mom confided that my dad planned to buy me a doll he had seen in our local five-and-dime store, I complained. And complained again.

My mother had a special gift for making an obviously less-than-ideal situation seem better than it actually was. Seeing my lack of enthusiasm she began to exercise her talent during the weeks before Christmas. She said, "It's not really the kind of doll you play with. A lot of teenage girls keep a doll on their bed as a room decoration. This doll is so big, it wears toddler size clothes, not doll clothes." And finally, "Your daddy says he wants to get you a doll for Christmas just one last time."

I understood that my mother didn't want to risk hurting my dad's feelings by trying to change his mind, and truthfully, neither did I. So I said nothing more about it. But I didn't rush out and tell my friends what I expected for Christmas. The closer the holidays approached, the more puzzled I became over that phrase, "just one last time." I didn't understand why, but for some reason this doll-thing seemed to be awfully important to my dad.

Every year on Christmas morning my brothers and I had our own special spot in the living room where we would find our Christmas presents laid out unwrapped. The first thing I saw that year when I looked at my end of the sofa was a big golden haired doll dressed in blue flannel pajamas. I tried to act reasonably pleased. After all, my stash included other more grown-up presents, too — a charm bracelet, clothes, and a white Bible with a little cross for a zipper pull.

Honestly, that doll didn't mean much for me on that Christmas morning so long ago. But like all presents given out of pure love, it grew more precious with time. The doll told me things that my quiet father never spoke in words. It told me that he loved me and I would always hold a special place in his heart. It hinted at the special bond between a daddy and his little girl — a bond that made a daddy want to buy his daughter a doll for Christmas "just one last time."

But these insights did not come quickly. They crystallized gradually as I watched my own little girl play with that same doll during visits to my parents' house. Then came the day when I first saw my granddaughter hugging the well-worn doll with the golden hair and blue pajamas. Finally, I understood the greatest lesson learned that Christmas: Sometimes we give to others by simply receiving from them.

~ *Dianne Neal Matthews*

❧ 43 ❧
The Birth That Saves

It's the season. The Hallmark channel entertains us with sweet Christmas stories that always end happily ever after. The Grinch even turns from his evil ways and realizes, "Christmas doesn't come from a store, maybe Christmas perhaps means a little bit more."

Starting the day after Thanksgiving, in addition to the enchanting array of sparkling lights and colorful decorations, holiday music surrounds us.

It's a happy time of year. We escape in the magic by decorating our homes, scenting the kitchen with the fragrance of gingerbread, shopping, and scattering the beautifully wrapped presents under the tree.

We celebrate Christmas.

Except when we can't.

Except when our hearts are breaking.

Except when the empty seat at the table reminds us that life is not happily ever after.

This season brings me to such a time. Each day I sit by my beloved aunt's bedside as she lies dying. My heart breaks at the thought of my world without her. She's always been my rock. The keeper of my soul. Light in the darkness. My love for her knows no bounds. I sit and wait for a voice that can no longer speak. Her love, however, breaks through the chains of disease and she drinks me in through her beautiful blue-grey eyes. She blinks three times — our code for, "I love you."

My beloved will be gone by Christmas. Her chair will be empty. Her laughter a memory. How can I possibly celebrate Christmas in a world without her kindness, love, and goodness? How can I celebrate Christmas?

Turning from my grief, I ask myself: How can I *not* celebrate Christmas?

What is Christmas but the gift of our God, who so loved the world he gave his only Son so that we may have eternal life. My aunt will live because he lives. She will go from sickness to fullness of life eternally in heaven with her Savior. It is only when we experience life's traumas through the filter of the power of the Cross that we can truly celebrate Christmas.

The empty chair will still be at the table on Christmas day, but it will be a reminder of life — a life still lived with the Savior she served. My tears will come, but Oswald Chambers reminds us that tears are the diamonds of heaven.

Christmas is a celebration of the birth that saves. Because Jesus came, died, and lives, we can face tomorrow.

~ Emme Gannon

~ 44 ~
Finding Baby Jesus

"Find the Baby Jesus," at Christmastime is not only a phrase uttered in our house as a mantra of remembering the reason for the season, but the name of a game which has been played in my husband's family for over thirty years.

The first year that I dated my husband, Andy, I was a seventeen-year-old college freshman who thought she was a very mature young woman. When visiting his parents' home during Christmas break, I realized just how much of a kid I still was.

One day when I arrived at their house, Andy's two teenage brothers — who usually popped out of their video-game-playing den just long enough to greet me with sweaty, adolescent hugs before quickly retreating once more to their stinky subterranean lair — were too busy making thudding and smashing noises upstairs to be bothered to come down and say hello.

The yelled dialogue between Andy's dad, who was trying to get his sons to be polite and say, "Hi," and the boys who didn't want to leave the upstairs area of the house because someone else would "find it," sounded intriguing enough that I moseyed on upstairs to see what the fuss was all about.

Accompanied by my then-boyfriend, I went upstairs to find not only the two teenagers, but also their fifty-something-year-old uncle, all rifling through different things in an upstairs bedroom.

One boy's hind quarters protruded from an attic eave as the hidden upper half of his body made suspicious-sounding thumping noises. The other boy was systematically and thoroughly going through every item in each drawer of a dresser. Their uncle lay on his belly, partially under a bed, flailing like a fish out of water while intermittently sneezing and coughing as he shoved items around.

I turned around to request clarification of the situation from my boyfriend, only to find him off in a corner, picking up trophies, turning them upside down, and shaking them. Any attempts at conversation with the males in the room were met with either grunts or, in the case of the uncle, sneezes.

Since no one upstairs could be bothered to give me an explanation as to this very odd behavior, I went downstairs to seek out the only apparently sane people in this house — Andy's parents. As Andy's dad reclined on a chair with a decidedly smug expression on his face, his mom explained to me what was going on upstairs.

After her children were born, Andy's mom decided she wanted her young sons to remember the reason for Christmas in the midst of all of the hustle and bustle that accompanies the holiday. To enforce that, she came up with a hide-and-seek game in which the Baby Jesus figurine from the family's nativity set was hidden somewhere new each day in December.

First, the nativity set was put in the kitchen on December 1. The boys knew that when Christmas was still a long way off, Baby Jesus would be hidden somewhere far away from the kitchen. As Christmas drew nearer, the figurine would be hidden in a closer location, moving from the upstairs bedrooms down to the kitchen. As the boys grew older, the hiding spots became more challenging.

"Since it's still a few weeks before Christmas," Andy's mom said, "Baby Jesus is hidden upstairs, far away from his manger."

She explained the rules of the game, which were simple. Andy's dad, a purported object-concealment genius, would hide Baby Jesus in the house. Anyone could search for Baby Jesus at any time. The location of the figurine was not to be shared with anyone else in the house. To ensure integrity, each successful finder of the figurine would go whisper the location to Andy's dad.

Andy's family, being just a wee bit competitive, would not only race to see who could find Baby Jesus first, but also in the least amount of time. I do not know what the record was, since discussion of this topic was a hotly contested subject matter. They also reveled in their Baby-Jesus-finding superiority over all amateurs who tried (often unsuccessfully) to find the figurine.

How hard could it be? I had played hide-and-seek as a kid, and was a master at finding objects buried under piles of dirty laundry, so finding a figurine should be a piece of cake. Right?

Boy, was I wrong.

Taking pity on the newbie, Andy's dad told me that Baby Jesus was indeed in the room in which the others were looking. He told me that after

Andy's extraordinarily smug-looking youngest brother sauntered downstairs, whispered in his dad's ear. When his dad nodded, the brother grinned and strutted back to the stinky-man-cave. So, I went upstairs and began my search.

Less than a minute after I had reached the room to search, Andy and his middle brother both triumphantly raced down the stairs. I later learned both had found the figurine before the youngest brother, but didn't want the other brother to see where it had been, so spent extra time trying to throw the other sibling off.

Twenty minutes later Andy's uncle gave a triumphant crow and ambled down the stairs.

An hour after I started my search, I was in tears. Poor Andy came back upstairs only to find his girlfriend bawling over not being able to find Baby Jesus.

Chuckling, he kindly reminded me that his brothers and he had played this game their whole lives, and that I had never done it before. I should do better next time. He then showed me where Baby Jesus was located. It was inside a rolled-up pair of socks, in the back of a drawer.

Seriously, who is supposed to find things hidden like that?

He said that was an "easy one."

In the weeks that followed, despite help from one of Andy's brothers, I could not find Baby Jesus. I now know the brother well enough to wonder if he actually was helping me, or just enjoying messing with me.

I am thinking the latter.

Andy and I carried this tradition on in our home so our children could experience the joy (and stress) of searching for and then finding Baby Jesus. And yes, I am still the last to find the figurine each time, soundly trounced by preschoolers and octogenarians alike.

This simple game has kept the reason for Christmas — the birth of the baby Jesus — forefront in our minds, reminding us, along with family and friends who join in, to find Baby Jesus, to persist in seeking after Him. It is a tradition I am very grateful my mother-in-law started, and one I hope our children will carry to their homes, as well.

~ *Marybeth Mitcham*

45

Are You There, Lord?

The second week in December, 2014, I awoke feeling the weight of the season. I love Christmas, but so many other things were happening in my life, primarily a loved one's illness and the added responsibilities that brought, that I was struggling to accomplish the normal routine, let alone the demands of the holiday. I was feeling squeezed almost to the breaking point.

I woke, as well, feeling the weight of the loss of an employee from my husband's business, a highly-advanced machine shop. Concerned what it would mean if the business was short-handed, I quickly offered a prayer requesting God bring us a skilled and eager young man, one who loved and followed the Lord.

I also thought of my son, his wife, and the grandchildren and their need to find a church to attend. With schooling and job moves, they had not been active in a fellowship for a number of years. The children were now in preschool; I longed for them to find a vibrant church to nourish them spiritually. I pray daily for their walk with the Lord, and for the grandchildren to someday accept Jesus as their Savior.

I knew I'd be lifting these issues again during my prayer time in a few minutes. So, I arose to begin my day.

I fixed my morning coffee and settled on the loveseat in the den, eager to lift my spirit by spending time with the Lord…reading his word, praying, and simply being still before him. As I took a satisfying sip of coffee and picked up my Bible, a surprising question literally popped into my mind, "Are you there, Lord?"

I was startled that I would ask such a question, knowing that, of course, as a believer and follower of Christ, God is always with me. Yet, even more surprising, I found myself asking a second time, "Are you *really* there?"

I remember smiling at the seeming foolishness of my questions as I opened the Word to read the chapter in Deuteronomy, where I happened to be in my journey through the Bible. Once that was completed, I opened my devotional book, *Dear Jesus* by Sarah Young, and turned to the bookmarked page and read:

Beloved, you are right on target. Openness to My Presence is all about faith: believing that though I am invisible, I am both Real and really with you.

Stunned, I reread the sentence, my mind whirling at this "coincidence." I continued reading…astonished and overwhelmed by God's message that particular morning, of all mornings. I dropped to my knees and prayed, humbled and awed by the mercy of this divine moment.

If my story ended here, that would have been remarkable enough, but God was not done revealing his divine presence and holiness to me that day.

My husband, Patrick, came home for our usual lunch together. About halfway through, he received a text message from his production manager, Brad. I was at the kitchen sink washing dishes when Patrick said, "Listen to this."

He proceeded to read that Brad was at lunch and had run into a young friend he'd known from a former church who was completing a machinist course at the community college in Asheville, North Carolina. This young man was looking for employment, and Brad had suggested he contact my husband for an interview.

Brad wrote very favorably about the young man, and Patrick was excited to meet him.

I listened, again stunned, and promptly burst into tears. I managed to say I had just prayed that morning for God to send a person who was a believer in Christ to replace the departing employee. After that, for at least five minutes, I was unable to speak another word.

The story of Zachariah, the father of John the Baptist, came to mind during this silence. He had been silent and unable to speak until John's birth, because he disbelieved the angel Gabriel's words to him that he and Elizabeth would have a son. I felt, perhaps, the same as he did: chastened by my own uncertainty, even fear at times, about how God would answer my prayers — chastened by my questions about God's very real presence and love for me, and for my family.

I continued to cry, overwhelmed by this amazing and immediate answer to prayer. I finally whispered, "I can't speak."

Patrick smiled and after a minute asked, "Do you know why the Lord did this?"

"For the shop," I mumbled softly.

He came over and put his arms around me and said, "No. You prayed about something else today, and the Lord answered this prayer so you would know he heard you and will answer the other part of your prayer, too. He wants you to know he will answer it in his time."

For many weeks afterward, I couldn't share this story without tears…tears for God's mercy on my life…tears for his mercy on my family…tears that he would come to me in such a dual way and reveal his amazing grace.

We were in the midst of the Christmas season when we celebrate the birth of Jesus Christ, the miracle of his arrival on earth, leading to the cross of Calvary, and I could barely grasp this truth: *Behold, the virgin shall be with child, and bear a Son, and they shall call His name Immanuel, which is translated, "God with us."* (Matthew 1:23 NKJV)

God with us, a thought so tremendous, a reality so riveting, I still have tears…and renewed hope…for God's witness is ever before me.

Patrick hired the young man, a believer who is capable, bright and talented. And within a month my son and his wife found a church for their family… our family — after all that time.

Prayer for those I love is ongoing and forever. It's part of every breath. Christmas is a reminder that answered prayer is promised to those who accept the miracle of the baby in the manger, the gift that is Jesus, born to be our Savior.

~ Ann Greenleaf Wirtz

❧ 46 ❦
Ghost of Christmas Past

Let me tell you what happened last night. I was lying in my bed, about to doze off, and I saw a light flicker under my bedroom door. I got out of bed cautiously, tiptoeing across the floor. I cracked the door open and what I saw made my heart skip fourteen beats!

I saw a ghost that was constantly changing. He would be normal one minute, and have four arms the next. He had a great light shining out of his head. As I trembled in fear I asked, "Who are you?"

He replied, "I am the Ghost of Christmas Past!"

I instantly knew what this meant. He was going to show me Christmases from my past. I had once read a book like this, but I couldn't remember the name of it. He looked at me and could tell I knew what was about to happen. He asked, "Are you ready?" My knees were knocking with fear as I let out an almost inaudible squeak, which he apparently took as a yes.

My surroundings faded away and I was suddenly at my Oma's house (oma is German for grandmother). I couldn't have been more than two years old. All of my family was there and even though I was the youngest, I was having fun. Uncles, aunts, Papa, Oma, and my cousins were there. I didn't remember much from this Christmas, but I instantly recognized one thing…Papa was there.

I hadn't seen his face in what seemed like an eternity, yet there he was, smiling and talking with everyone. I knew something that everyone in that room didn't know — this would be our last Christmas with Papa. I begged the Spirit to let me watch the scene longer, but he denied me, cruelly.

That 2002 Christmas faded and a new Christmas appeared. There I was at age four, at Oma's house again. There was still some sort of cheer, but the overall mood was sorrowful. There was a chill in the air, as if someone had left a window open all day in the dreary North Carolina weather. But there was no doubt in my mind that it was an empty seat that had belonged to someone we all loved deeply in our hearts. Papa wasn't there.

I was a little confused, but I don't know if I truly understood why he wasn't there. This time I begged the Spirit to leave this Christmas, but he lingered there just long enough for my sorrow to build.

Then he showed me brief glimpses of my next five Christmases. They were filled with joy and laughter. Friends and family would come over and we would have a great time. I had found a sport I loved and I had made a goal to achieve. Those five years were truly amazing. Then he showed me the most heartbreak I had ever had.

He made me experience it again and I loathed the Ghost for it. What he showed me at first wasn't Christmas Day, but May 31, 2010. I had been at Oma's house all day when my parents showed up. I could tell something wasn't right, but I was afraid to ask what it was. Then they told me that Grandpa had died. I was old enough to understand everything this time.

At first, I was too furious to cry. All I could think was, "WHY?!" I was beside myself as I went to the car and slammed my water bottle down. Then we went to Grandma's house, and my heart was broken for two reasons: We'd already lost Papa. Now Grandpa, and the fact that Grandma had lost him. I sobbed for what seemed like thirty minutes. Why was the Ghost showing me this? Had I done something to deserve this horrible curse of having to relive this heartache? The scene of me crying in a bedroom faded away to that year's Christmas. The mood was dampened by the empty rocking chair. It was dampened without the, "Grandpa, open your present!"

Then I was back in my own bedroom again. The scenery had changed so fast I thought I might throw up. The room was dark and my bedroom door was closed. It was almost as if the Ghost of Christmas Past had never come, but I knew he had. Dreams were never that vivid. Dreams were never that painful.

I hated that Ghost with so much passion. I remembered in which book I had read about him. It was *A Christmas Carol*. I found the book and burned it. It had been a good story, but it had happened to me now, and that made *A Christmas Carol* about as delightful as sour milk. I went back to bed exhausted.

Whether I liked it or not, I thought about what the Spirit had showed me. Then I knew what the meaning was. Spend time with loved ones and live with no regrets. I suppose that's what his reason was, of showing me all of that.

So, here I am, writing this journal about last night. But I have learned from this experience...so excuse me for a moment...

I think I'll go give my cousin a call.

~ *Simon Wilson* (written when age 14)

❧ 47 ❧
Presence for Christmas

The Saturday before Christmas, exhaustion hit, replacing the joy of Christmas with anxiety. I sat on the floor of my bedroom, surrounded with mountains of presents still to wrap, not to mention the long list of to-dos still waiting to be done. I knew it was my job to make sure my family had a memorable Christmas — focused on Jesus — but I just couldn't see how to make that happen.

Somewhere along the path from Thanksgiving to Christmas, I had lost my focus. Everywhere I looked, the season seemed shallow and meaningless. If I couldn't find God in the season, how was I going to make sure my three boys found him? All I could do was pray. It wasn't even a very good prayer — more like a cry for help.

Almost before I said, "Amen," our oldest son, an energetic seven-year-old, knocked on my door. "Can we all go Christmas-light-looking tonight, please?"

I mentally groaned. Something else to do. Not exactly an answer to prayer. I slipped out of my room, making sure I kept him from seeing the presents. "I don't think so. I have too much to do."

"Pleasssssse?" He drew the word out, and his two little brothers joined the chorus, bringing their dad in from the living room.

I didn't want to disappoint them, and if they were out of the house I could play catch up. "Maybe your dad can take you without me?" I turned pleading eyes to my husband.

Neither he nor the boys were buying into the idea. My husband put a comforting arm around me and leaned to whisper into my ear. "I'll help you later. This is important." He turned to the boys. "I think it's a wonderful idea, and we'll all go, even your mom."

We did go that night. The five of us crowded into our ancient minivan. As we drove around, I listened to the excited exclamations of my boys and realized God had answered my prayer. He'd helped me by showing me that what needed to get done would get done. More importantly, I needed to seek out the real part of Christmas and let it change my perspective, remembering that the meaning of Christmas isn't found in presents, but in the presence of both God and my family.

~ Edie Melson

48

Come Dance with Me

It was our second Christmas together. As a young couple starting out in life, finances were tight. We agreed not to spend money on presents for each other that holiday. Instead, we would give each other a gift that did not cost money.

For a couple of weeks I considered what to give my lovely wife. Finally it came to me. I would write her a song.

The words came easily. Her beautiful spirit and the young love we shared made me want to dance in her arms again and again.

I had asked Tracey to marry me while we stood high in the steeple of Alumni Chapel overlooking the campus of The Southern Baptist Theological Seminary in Louisville, Kentucky. Now almost two years later on Christmas Eve, we sat down on the couch in our rented house and shared our gifts with each other. When it was my turn, I led her by the hand to the piano in the sunroom. Sitting down, I played and sang her Christmas gift. To this day it is one of my favorite gifts I ever gave.

> Tracey Alane, how lovely is your name
> How soft and pretty are your hands and face
> When I hold you, time stands still like a child on Christmas morn'
> And when we kiss, my heart just seems to be at home

Chorus:
> Come dance with me through the changes of life's seasons
> Share with me your laughter and all your life will bring
> And when life is over and our work on earth has ended
> We'll know we danced and we had a song to sing

> Up in that steeple I asked you to dance with me
> And when you said yes, our music was just starting
> As we descend into the shadows of life's steeples,
> May we not forget the love that made us one

It is King Jesus who made us for each other
And let us hear the music flowing from His heart
May we be filled with the knowledge of His great love
As we walk hand in hand may we dance with Him.

~ Dr. Rhett H. Wilson

～ 49 ～
Am I Good Enough?

"Have you been a good little girl this year?"

I heard this time and time again when I was a child, along with statements such as: "If you've been naughty instead of nice, you'll get coal in your stocking instead of candy."

When I answered, "Yes, I've been good," I was surely hoping "good enough" would get me presents instead of nasty coal.

These are typical things adults say to children as Christmas approaches. Maybe it's because we don't really know what else to say. Christmas is a wonderful time, and Santa makes things fun and exciting for all of us — along with the other traditions of the holiday season. But as I hear these comments more and more, it makes me wonder what we're really teaching our children about life…and especially about God.

Looking back and remembering how much I struggled with self-esteem — always feeling I didn't measure up to the standard of others — I wonder if trying to be *good* for Santa caused me to grow up thinking I had to be *good* for God or he wouldn't bless me…or even love me.

Because children think they have to earn Santa's approval in order to get gifts from him, do they grow up thinking the same thing about a loving heavenly Father? Actually, as adults how many of us have that same mentality? Do we boldly approach the throne of grace as the Word says, or do we shy away from God, believing we haven't met the mark?

If this is something you struggle with, let me share some scriptural truth I've learned along the way:

God is for me. He is on my side.

He promises to do battle for me when necessary.

I am saved by grace, not by what I do.

He covers me with his robe of righteousness.

He calls me his child, his chosen, his beloved.

He forgives me when I fail and strengthens me when I'm weak.

He does not play favorites; what he's done for others, he'll do for me.

He accepts me exactly the way I am, but loves me too much to leave me that way.

He has delivered me from guilt, shame, and condemnation.

He has seated me in heavenly places with Christ.

He sees me perfect and complete in him.

My name is engraved in the palm of his hand.

His faithfulness is never failing, and his mercies are new every morning.

In every situation, his grace is sufficient for me.

Child of God, during the Christmas season — and every other day of the year — know that your Father loves you, is intimately acquainted with you, and has a wonderful plan and purpose for your life. You don't ever have to worry about being good enough. *Only God is truly good,* and he loves you with an unconditional, everlasting love.

- Andrea Merrell

❧ 50 ❧

Suzy Snowflake and the Blue Christmas that Turned White

The front door had been wrapped like a present and was garnished with a bow. All of our received Christmas cards had been taped on the inside of the door to form a Christmas tree. A pine tree's scent permeated the entire house while red, blue, and yellow bubble lights rested on limbs of evergreen glittering with silver icicles and holding more than one ornament. Striped ribbon candy decorated ruby red dishes not far from a basket laden with crisp apples, oranges, and mixed nuts waiting to be cracked to reveal tasty meats. Elvis could be heard crooning "Blue Christmas" from the stereo.

In the dining room, the table was graced with a nutmeg scored ham straight from the oven and groaned even more from the weight of vegetables, rolls, cakes, and pies of all shapes and sizes — all made from scratch at the request of family members.

In the front yard, the doll I'd named Darlene — the doll who was my childhood best friend — was on display next to the sign "Suzy Snowflake." That song title had been one of the few Christmas song titles left for Mother to choose from the neighborhood garden club's list. Residents were supposed to use that list for decorations.

Songs like "Jingle Bells," "Away in a Manger," and "Silver Bells" — all titles that would have been easy to find decorations for — had already been taken by women who participated in the garden club. Since Mother worked and couldn't attend meetings which were held during work hours, the titles left to choose from were slim pickings.

"I've never even heard of 'Suzy Snowflake,'" I said, fuming when it was suggested by other family members that one of my dolls could be used for Suzy. Why did *I* have to make the sacrifice? Why did my Darlene have to be the sacrifice?

"Anyone else have any better ideas?" Mother asked.

No one did. Nor did I.

So, against my fervent wishes, I finally acquiesced and allowed Darlene to pretend to be Suzy Snowflake. Dressed in a winter coat, hat, scarf, gloves, and red rubber boots, she was to stand in the damp dark cold 'til midnight — eyes opened wide and never blinking, snowflakes piling all around her — while silently offering a semi-beauty queen wave to all the cars filled with Christmas decoration gawkers.

Those were families, much like mine, who for at least one night during the two weeks of Christmas celebrations, made their rounds from neighborhood to neighborhood, their tires' snow chains nipping rubber while chinking and jangling against the snow-covered asphalt, to view the sights.

"It's okay," I told Darlene, planting her boots in the snow and pulling her neck scarf tighter to keep her warm. "You're a real trooper. You're only acting as Suzy Snowflake, kind of like a movie star playing a character in a movie. Be brave. Don't be scared. It's only until midnight and then I'll bring you inside. You can sleep with me to warm up before going out again tomorrow. And if anyone tries to kidnap you, scream bloody murder. What don't we do for this family of ours? Talk about a blue Christmas."

I kissed her goodbye and trudged back to the house, miserable at having to leave my best friend out in the freezing weather, pretending to be a flaky snowflake. Surely Darlene and I could get through this, but I was blue. Christmas was not meant to be blue. People dreamed of white Christmases… white symbolized purity and kindness. Blue symbolized…sadness.

During the ensuing nights leading up to Christmas, I slept next to the coldest piece of plastic ever molded on planet earth. But by morning, Darlene was always ready to take her place outside next to her "Suzy Snowflake" sign, never complaining. She had a perpetual smile on beautiful full lips, as if willing and ready to be a sacrificial flake.

A few nights later, most of our extended family gathered inside our toasty warm home for our big family meal. Other than Darlene, who was doing her duty outside, there was one person missing who sometimes spent Christmas with us. Cousin Charles. Granddaddy's namesake.

He'd been making his own sacrifices while fighting in the jungles of Vietnam and had been wounded by friendly fire that left a huge crater in his back. After serving his country, he'd been flown back to a Texas hospital where doctors used every skill they had been gifted with to save him.

His sacrifice had been tremendous. His recovery arduous — and early on fairly grim. Even though we'd exchanged only a couple of letters during the war, I'd missed him something fierce when his letters stopped coming.

He'd been the older cousin who'd set up a Santa's sweat shop in the living room to put together my Barbie Doll Dream House when Santa had dropped it off but forgot to assemble it. He'd been the cousin to gift me with Barbie's navy blue airline stewardess outfit — my favorite gift that year. And he'd been the cousin who'd pointed out to me one Christmas that Santa had not only made a mistake in bringing me an electric guitar with no amp instead of an acoustic guitar, but Santa had also forgotten that Charles couldn't eat chocolates and had left him an entire box. So, I wasn't the only one who thought Santa was losing his edge and becoming forgetful.

This blue Christmas evening, we all had Charles on our minds as Uncle Roy said the prayer and blessed the food. Waiting in line to heft ham onto his plate before dipping into the sweet potatoes, Daddy stepped back to look out the picture window. "A car stopped," he said. "Looks like the driver has opened his door. Wonder who that could be?"

"Probably someone with car trouble or no snow chains," said Granddaddy.

I ran outside. Even though she was a redhead with lots of spunk, Darlene was still a doll and couldn't save herself…and no one was running off with my best friend — the gift Santa had brought me when I was in third grade and had asked for a three-year-old-brunette doll. Darlene and I had made all the sacrifices we were going to make this Christmas.

I kept my eyes on the would-be thief who slowly unfolded himself and eased out of the low-slung sports car. Tall and thin, he held onto the car's door for balance. He reminded me of someone. But no one I knew acted that ancient and could still drive.

When he turned to me and grinned, I knew he wasn't there to kidnap Darlene.

"Surprise!" he called. "Merry Christmas."

That voice…Charles! He didn't look like the young man who'd left for war, but like someone weary. Battle-worn. With his wound packed and bandaged, he'd been allowed to come home. He'd made it as far as Tennessee to be with extended family for our annual Christmas dinner before trekking home to North Carolina.

"You're here. I can't believe it! You're really here!" I turned to the pretend Suzy Snowflake. "Darlene! It's Charles!"

"Bet you thought you'd never see *me* again," said Charles, his comment followed by that infectious laugh of his. "What's with the doll?"

Even though he'd been at death's door — a huge chunk of him still missing — he hadn't lost his sarcastic wit. And he'd come home. Not totally whole, but on the mend. Available if Santa forgot to assemble any more presents.

I ran back to the house and saw Daddy and my uncles pouring out the front door.

"It's Charles!" I shouted "He's really here!"

I thought about sacrifices. About Jesus and the real reason we celebrate Christmas to remember his birthday, along with his being the sacrificial lamb who gave all. He had answered our prayers and was still performing a healing work in our soldier.

Indeed, the trooper who had sacrificed for all of us had finally made it home. The real trooper — no snowflake. And just in time to help turn my blue Christmas totally white.

~ *Vicki H. Moss*

❧ 51 ❧
From My Heart to Theirs

It was late October, but many people coming out of the early church service carried a shoebox decorated for Christmas. *What a great idea!* I thought when I learned that our church was sponsoring Operation Christmas Child — the Samaritan's Purse project that provides Christmas gifts for children all over the world. That kind of project had sparked my interest for years, and now the church made it easy for me to participate.

I quickly grabbed two of the three hundred boxes. Shopping was fun as I thought about the girl who would carry the pink sequin purse or the boy who would spend hours trying to figure out the secret of the Rubik's Cube. Practical items such as tools, socks, soap and washcloths filled up the boxes. Of course there had to be jewelry for the girl and a ball for the boy. I began to feel a connection with the children.

The instructions that came with the box said to pray for the child, include a letter or note, and a picture. Instead of praying *for* the child, I decided to pray *with* the child. For each child, I cut out eight hearts on which I wrote prayers. When they were finished, I stapled them at the two top arches to form a booklet. The title page read: Prayers for a Special Girl/Boy. I then quoted Jeremiah 29:13, the scripture that inspired the idea of the hearts: *You will seek me and find me when you seek for me with all your heart.* (NIV)

My first prayer was one of thanks for sending Jesus to be our Savior and Friend. I prayed, "Thank you for the privilege of sharing Christmas with my new friend — this precious boy. May he find as much joy in receiving this gift as I found in putting it together."

The true celebration of Christmas is more than a one-day event. It's a godly lifestyle created by forming a relationship with God, made possible through the death and resurrection of Jesus Christ. I prayed that the children would experience an encounter with Jesus that would changes their lives.

Anticipating some of the needs of preteens and teens, I covered various situations with prayer. Since the gifts were going to disadvantaged children,

I knew there would be times of serious need — perhaps when they would be without food and other life essentials. I prayed that God would send someone to fill the need. "Help her to feel your love and to trust in you."

Prayers about school were meant to inspire the children with a desire to learn and develop good study habits. "Help him to prepare to become the person you want him to be."

For emotional situations, I prayed, "If someone is unkind to my friend, help her turn to you for healing of the pain. Because I can't be there for her, hug her heart for me. Help her to pray for the one who hurt her. As she prays, she will be able to let go of her anger and forgive the offender. Through forgiveness she will find healing."

My final prayer focused on the value of thanksgiving. "When something good happens to my friend, help him to realize that all good things come from you. Help him experience the peace and joy that come from a thankful heart."

I felt good when the project was completed, but I wondered if my prayers would actually connect with the recipients. For instance, how could we get through the language barrier?

It was as though God answered my question. While surfing through television channels, I caught an interview with Franklin Graham, president of Samaritan's Purse. I learned more about the program and saw a video of children receiving the gifts.

Gifts would be distributed at churches where leaders could possibly interpret the prayers. But if there fails to be human interaction, I trust the Holy Spirit to connect the prayers from my heart to the hearts of the children.

The project gave me an early start on the celebration of the most wonderful time of the year. After my cancer surgery on December 1, 1999, Christmas became more precious to me even without the usual trappings. Through the years, I have continued to focus on the more important aspects of the season rather than the things that sap my energy.

Now, through my giving to children, I have yet another tradition to enhance my joy in remembering the Savior's birth.

~ Esther M. Bailey

You Are Christmas

You are
the Messiah
they prayed for.
Your light
shined one starry night,
and gave great joy
to a world in need of a Savior.

You are
Christmas Present.
God with us.
Your word
washes over us,
and covers our hearts
when blizzards rage.

You are
the Giver
who gave everything.
Your truth
gives us hope,
and helps us see
Christmas Miracles are real.

You are
the Prince Of Peace,
strength in our weakness.
Your life
lived selflessly
gives us wings
to fly ever free.

You are
the Gift
I always craved.
Your heart
is my home,
and song.
Father, God, Jesus,
You are Christmas.

- Joann Claypoole

53

Christmas Retreat

I needed to escape. My days were churning together in an endless swirl of busyness. I was drowning in the tasks of Christmas preparation rather than soaking in the peacefulness of its meaning. I had to do something before I was completely sucked under, unable to breathe.

So on Sunday afternoon, I decided to take a drive to visit a special friend. I had not seen Laura since October, but I knew I would find the peace I was looking for in her presence. My friend Laura is a singer, songwriter and musician. Her Christmas concert at the Union Coffee House promised to be the refocusing element I so desperately needed.

My journey took me down winding roads sandwiched between dirty brown farm fields, plowed and tucked away for the upcoming winter snow. Houses and barns dotted the roadside as I wound through the vast open country. While I drove, the thoughts that cluttered my mind when I left soon began to evaporate. The further from home I wandered, the clearer my mind became. My focus shifted to the impending concert and the rejuvenation I hoped it would bring.

As I arrived in the serene little town, I found the coffee house nestled on the corner of two streets. On its outside, all was quiet and still. Yet when I opened the door, my ears were greeted with a cacophony of conversation and the gargling grind of an espresso machine. Baristas bustled behind the counter. The aroma of maple nut coffee hung heavy in the air, tickling my nose with an invitation to partake. The coffee house walls bulged with people who had come, just like me, to indulge in a Sunday afternoon retreat. I stepped to the counter, purchased a Mocha Chiller, and then found a seat at a front row table.

Through Laura's music, for the next hour and a half I was transported into the land of Bethlehem and the birth of the Christ child. The melody of old familiar Christmas carols enwrapped me like a warm blanket. Her original compositions made my heart long for family. Some songs thrust me into the realm of worshiping the baby born to save the world. I closed my eyes, listening contentedly as Laura passionately sang of our Savior. I had finally found the peace for which my soul ached. In that short span of time, my heart was born anew.

When Laura's concert ended, I chatted with her briefly before making my way home. Having arrived with a heavy heart burdened by the tasks of the season, I departed with my heart renewed, refocused on the joy Christmas brings. My mind was centered, once again, on the reason we celebrate Christmas. The birth of Jesus Christ our Savior.

As this Christmas approaches, find a moment to step away from the busyness of the season and retreat to a quiet place. Spend some time reflecting on the birth of Christ. When you do, perhaps you will find the peace you long for and your heart will be renewed.

- Sheryl Baker

∽ 54 ∾
Poor Baby Jesus

My four-year-old grandson, Drew, turned a clear round plastic ornament until the manger inside it was upright. Inside the manger was Baby Jesus on a few loose strands of straw.

"Look Nana, I made this at church," Drew said. "It's Baby Jesus."

"Baby Jesus," Drew's two-year-old sister, Annalise, echoed.

"Oh Drew, it's beautiful!" I said.

"I'll show you something else I made," Drew said, pointing to the floor. "Sit down."

I sat on the blue-carpeted floor beside Annalise. We watched as Drew pulled crinkled drawings, popsicle-stick figures, and other treasures from his box, showed them to us, and laid each one on the floor.

Annalise held onto the plastic ornament, and each time Drew showed us something new, Annalise lifted the ornament up and said, "Baby Jesus." He was clearly her favorite of Drew's treasures.

When lunch time rolled around, I told Drew that we needed to clean up before going downstairs. "We'll help you," I said.

Drew crawled around, picking up his papers and stick figures. Annalise had laid the ornament down so I rolled it across the floor to Drew.

Annalise rushed to get it. She picked it up, held it close to her little body, glared at me and said, "Poor Baby Jesus." My causing Baby Jesus to tumble over and over was not acceptable to her.

Feeling properly reprimanded by this two-year-old, I crawled over to Annalise, looked into the ornament, and said, "I'm sorry, Baby Jesus."

My apology was intended to appease Annalise, but sitting there on my knees, I felt a true pang of sorrow in my heart. In a precious moment, my grandchildren had shared with me their love and awe of Baby Jesus. In my haste to clean up, I completely forgot about the significance of the ornament and treated it like a scrap of paper or popsicle stick.

Many times during the Christmas season, I do that. I set out the manger scene, and get caught up with decorating, shopping, and baking. And I toss poor baby Jesus to the back of my mind.

This season, I want to hold this baby in my heart, just the way Annalise held him in her hand. When I decorate my tree, I want to remember — Baby Jesus.

When I buy a gift for a loved one, I want to remember — Baby Jesus.

When I bake goodies for my family, I want to remember — Baby Jesus.

And when the Christmas season is over, and it's time to clean up, I don't want to toss Baby Jesus across the floor. I want to carry him in my heart into the New Year.

~ Susan Dollyhigh

❧ 55 ❦
Setting Goals

We can easily get caught up in the Christmas season and before we realize it, the New Year will be here. Think about your life and goals you had last year. Did you meet them? Do you have goals for this coming year? Whether you make specific goals for a New Year or just strive to learn, grow, and produce according to your abilities, consider that the coming year may be a new beginning or greater effort of enriching your life.

One of my goals is to make a daily writing schedule (which I have to do when on deadline) and stick to it as much as possible. Also, I want to study the many books I have on the craft of writing. I easily get caught up in writing and leave little time for reading. I'm adding that to my goal — read more of the great books with which I surround myself.

The above is a paraphrased version of what I posted on a writers loop for responses. Below are some excerpted suggestions that might be of help to each of us.

1. Gain a clear understanding of your goal and what you want to achieve.
2. Have a timeline for when you want to complete your goal (someday is not one of the days of the week).
3. Find someone to keep you accountable and moving forward.
4. Get out of the house. Go to a coffee shop or if you need quiet go to a library.
5. If days are filled with work (at home or otherwise) get up an hour early for working on a project.
6. Learn to say "No" to a lot of activities that aren't fulfilling.
7. Manage time better.
8. Have a goal of "making goals."
9. Be sure your calendar indicates time for pleasure.
10. Without goals it's easy to spin one's wheels and waste time.

One person said her year was filled with surprises and new relationships because she made goals. She didn't reach them all, but achieved more than if she had not made the goals.

Another gave a response we could do before making our goals: Set apart a time in December to pray, draw near to God and hear what the Holy Spirit is saying regarding our goals.

One of my goals over a year ago was to volunteer some of my time in giving back to the Billy Graham organization since my writing career started in the 1980's at the Billy Graham School for Christian Writers. That conference opened up a whole new world for me.

When I felt I should volunteer, I told myself I didn't have time. When aspiring writers tell me they don't have time to write, I reply that they must make time. I realized if I really wanted to show my appreciation, then I would follow my own advice and make time to volunteer.

On many Saturday mornings, I now go to the Chapel at the Billy Graham Training Center, also known as The Cove. My favorite part is leading the tour through the sanctuary and up to the prayer room.

Just being there in that beautiful, elegant, simple, profound place high in the mountains, surrounded by trees and foliage, is a spiritual experience. There is no way I can begin to give anything near the blessings I receive by being there a few hours on a Saturday morning, relating to visitors who come from all over the nation and even from other countries.

There's a special feeling in that prayer room when people kneel at the round table in the center of which is a lighted globe, beneath the slant of the ceiling making a point beneath an eighty-seven-feet tall steeple and an eight-feet tall cross, symbolizing our need to pray for the world, and that our prayers go up to our Father in heaven — the one who sent his Son, Jesus, whose birthday we celebrate at Christmas.

I've learned that when I make a goal to give, not to receive, the blessings flow! And I can even be a blessing to others.

Merry Christmas, Happy New Year, and God Bless!

- Yvonne Lehman

About the Authors

Charlotte Adelsperger is an author and speaker from Overland Park, Kansas where she lives with her husband Bob. She has written four books and material for more than 200 publications and compilations. Her poetry has appeared in numerous magazines and gift books. Charlotte writes for both adults and children. Most recent is her children's picture book, *Amazing Miracles of Jesus*, illustrated by Nancy Munger, Tyndale House Publishers. Charlotte co-authored with her daughter, Karen Hayse, *Through the Generations: The Unique Call of Motherhood*.

Julie Arduini is author of the Amazon bestseller, *Entrusted* and co-author of *The Love Boat Bachelor* and *Unlikely Merger*. She also shared her story in the Amazon bestselling infertility devotional, *A Walk in the Valley*. She's the fiction contributing editor for the digital magazine, *Imaginate*, and blogs every other Wednesday for Christians Read. She resides in Ohio with her husband and two children. Learn more by visiting her at juliearduini.com or on Facebook at Julie Arduini.

Esther M. Bailey is a freelance writer who has a passion to share the good news of Jesus Christ. Living in Scottsdale, Arizona, she attends McDowell Mountain Community Church. In her leisure time, she enjoys Internet shopping, entertaining friends, and dining out.

Cathy Baker is an award-winning writer who delights in observing God at work in the nuances of life. Her work has been published in *Chicken Soup for the Soul*, *The Upper Room*, Focus on the Family's *Thriving Family* and others. Her award-winning poetry has appeared in two anthologies. She is also a regular contributor to *Inspire A Fire* and is a member of Cross N Pens, as well as the Light Brigade. With four grandchildren, a mustached-laden husband, a spoiled pooch named Rupert, and a 1963 Shasta Airflyte called Buttercup, she considers life to be quite the adventure. Visit her website: cathybaker.org

Sheryl Baker is a wife, mother, and grandmother. She lives in northwest Indiana with her husband, Ben. During the day she works as a customer service specialist. In her spare time, she loves to write. Sheryl is a published writer who enjoys bringing hope and encouragement through God's word. Her devotions have appeared in *Power for Today*, *Light from the Word*, and christiandevotions.us. Her story, "Mollie's Tale," is included in *Spoken*

Moment. She also maintains a weekly blog *Spun by the Potter: Discovering God in Everyday Life.* To see more of Sheryl's writing, visit spunbythepotter.com.

Dan Balow joined the Steve Laube Agency in July 2013 as a Literary Agent and Director of Publishing Development. He started working in publishing in 1983 and over the last 30+ years has been involved with the business side of the industry in marketing, sales, rights management, foreign sales, audio books, digital publishing, web management and acquisitions. Dan has developed a wide-ranging perspective on the industry, taken from involvement with hundreds of authors, thousands of books, and a love for the business. He served on the executive board of the trade association for Christian publishers in the U.S., is a founding member of the advisory board of the Christy Awards and is involved in training and mentoring Christian publishers around the world through Media Associates International. He holds a degree in Communications from Wheaton College. He and his wife Carol, a speech therapist in the public schools, live in Wheaton, Illinois. They have four grown children and one grandchild.

Carole A. Bell is a Licensed Professional Counselor whose ministry is empowering families to raise godly children in a secular world. Carole brings to her ministry knowledge and understanding from a wide range of experiences. She worked with special needs children and diverse cultural populations. She taught and counseled a broad variety of children and teens from the disinterested and discouraged to the eager learner and the gifted. In all of these children, she saw a common thread: the need to feel valued and empowered by the people in their lives. Her 32-year career in public education included counseling at all grade levels. She has worked 16 years as consultant and counselor in private practice as well as writer, speaker, and trainer in parenting issues. Her writings include a weekly Christian Parenting column for *Plainview Herald* since 1999 and a monthly column for *Hale Center Insider* since 2011. Her article, "The Tiny Waist of the Fifites" appears in *Chicken Soup for the Soul, Say Hello to a Better Body! Weight Loss and Fitness for Women Over 50.* Her website is ParentingfromtheSource.com.

Lisa Braxton is completing her first novel. Her stories have been published in *Chicken Soup for the Soul, Vermont Literary Review, The Sun* magazine and other literary journals, magazines, and anthologies.

Elsie H. Brunk and her husband of 56 years have four children, 12 grandchildren, and four great-grandchildren. Elsie has kept a journal for many years and is writing journals for each of her grandchildren. Her devotionals and articles have been published in *Christian Parenting Today, Live, The Family Digest, Standard, The Secret Place,* and other periodicals. Her book, *Encouragement in the Wilderness — Devotionals for Days of Discouragement, Depression, and Despair* was published in May 2002. In 2011, the book was published by Lighthouse Publishing of the Carolinas as an e-book titled, *Streams of Living Water for a Thirsty Soul.* Elsie's stories, "Grandchild Journal — Legacy of Love," and "The Roses" are included in *Precious, Precocious Moments.* Visit Elsie on her website at elsiehbrunk.com or contact her at ebrunk@rica.net.

Rebecca Carpenter writes at her lake retreat near Orlando. After retiring from teaching elementary school, she and her husband traveled the world for missions and pleasure. Time with her granddaughters, travel, and nature shape her writings, which have been published in local magazines, newspapers, compilations, and online. Her real-life devotionals give encouragement and hope. After losing her husband and parents in one year, writing devotionals about the grief helped in her healing and also comforted others in their difficult situations. Visit her blog: rebeccacarpenter.blogspot.com.

Joann M. Claypoole is the author of *DoveStories,* a children's chapter book series (ages 6-8), And *The Gardener's Helpers* (Morgan James Publishing). She has written a children's devotional book, *Coo Says You Are Loved* (ages 2-5). Her story, "A Picture in the Sky," is included in *Divine Moments.* Joann co-wrote the TV documentary script, *My Last Hope,* hosted by Candace Cameron-Bure, for National House of Hope (2011). Her inspirational prayers were featured on Clickandpray.com and have been compiled into two books, *All I Am* and *Everything to Me.* She also writes songs, voiceovers, plays, articles, and blogs. Joann is a member of the Christian Writers Guild, Word Weavers International (Orlando Chapter), SCBWI, Mt. Dora SCBWI Critique group, and Amhurst Writers and Critique Group. She is a wife, mother of four sons, Numi to three grandbabies, doggie-mom of two, and salon/spa owner in sunny Florida. Joann serves local and international missions and loves to sing on the praise and worship leading team at her local church.

Carlitta Cole-Kelly is a nurse, writer and author of two family history books. Her articles and short stories have appeared in *The Upper Room,* the UND *Alumni Review,* the 2015 award-winning *American River Review* literary journal, and *Gospel Roads* magazine. She was a co-honoree in 2006 for creative concepts included in the design of California's Medi-Cal logo.

Autumn Conley spent many of her years working in various offices but escaped Cubicle Land in 2009 to become a full-time freelance book editor. Writing has been a lifelong passion for Autumn, who began her writing career at the age of fourteen. Over the years, she has penned many essays, short stories, poems, and articles and has been published in anthologies such as *Chicken Soup*, *Soul Matters for Mothers*, *The Bad Hair Day Book*, and in magazines such as *Home Life*, *All You*, *New Moon for Girls*. Her children's story, "Where Does the Snow Go?," was accepted for publication in *Primary Treasures*. She self-published a suspense novella and a Christian teen novel, and is working on a new novel. In addition to writing and editing, Autumn busies herself with geocaching, a hobby that helps her enjoy the great outdoors with family and friends. She lives in Ohio, with her daughter, Cissy, and three small dogs. Contact Autumn at autiej@gmail.com or visit her on Facebook at ajcediting

Diana Derringer writes for several publications. She serves with her husband as a friendship family to international university students and treasures the gift of every day. Visit her at dianaderringer.com.

Susan Shelton Dollyhigh is a freelance writer and speaker. She is a contributing author in *Spirit and Heart: A Devotional Journey*, *Faith and Finances: In God We Trust*, *The Ultimate Christian Living*, *God Still Meets Needs*, and *I Believe in Heaven*. Susan's articles have appeared in *Connection Magazine*, *Exemplify Magazine*, *Mustard Seed Ministry*, *P31 Woman*, *The Upper Room* and *The Secret Place*.

Janet Perez Eckles makes inspiration dance into the heart of her readers and audiences as she incorporates her own triumph over heartache and tragedy. In her four books, articles, stories in dozens of anthologies, and from the stage or pulpit, Janet empowers and delights her English and Spanish-speaking audiences. Although blind, she teaches others to see the best of life through Christ's eyes. Visit her at janetperezeckles.com.

Sandra Fischer taught high school English and owned a Christian bookstore in Indiana before retiring and devoting time to writing. Many of her stories are gleaned from her experiences growing up in the Midwest. She has been published in *Guideposts*, various anthologies, *Faithwriters Magazine* online and on the Faithwriters.com website. Sandra lives in South Carolina with husband, Craig. To learn more about her and her writing visit her Amazon Author Page, or her bio at faithwriters.com.

Emme Gannon loves writing stories that stir the heart. She has written for Focus on the Family as well as numerous devotions. Her writing has received awards four consecutive years at the Blue Ridge Mountains Christian Writers Conference, including the Award of Excellence in Christian Literature. Emme just completed her first novel.

Theresa Jenner Garrido was born and raised in the beautiful Pacific Northwest. She spent the first nine years of her life on an island in Puget Sound, off the coast of Washington State. She attended the University of Washington, received a B.A. in English, and spent the next twenty-plus years teaching middle school language arts, social studies and drama before an early retirement. Theresa is now happy to indulge her wild imagination and passionate love of history — rooted in a deep faith in God — and share these foibles and gifts with others, including her husband, her ever-growing family, a rescue pup and the stray black cat that adopted her. Theresa has made her home in Missouri, Georgia, and North Carolina but currently resides in South Carolina. When not at the computer or vacuuming up pet hair, she enjoys traveling and poking her nose into strange and mysterious places.

Bernadean J. Gates retired after teaching third graders in a rural school district in Oklahoma for 33 years and moved to her parents' farm where she assists her mother as a caregiver to her ninety-six-year-old father as he recovers from a stroke. She assumed the daily care of her parents' small herd of cattle. She has articles published in *Mature Living, Teachers of Vision,* and *The Vision.* Some of her devotions have appeared online at christiandevotions.us. In September of 2013, she began a weekly-published blog, *Faith_Family_Farm* (bernadeanjgates.bogspot.com), to share family history as well as her faith and farm life.

Carol Graham teaches and shares the art of becoming a survivor based on her own traumatic life experiences. Her motto "laughter can get you through almost anything" helped her be a winner over cancer, rape, marital abuse, the false imprisonment of her husband, loss of a child, attempted suicide, and financial ruin. Her fast paced memoir, *Battered Hope,* is a story of hope, perseverance, and faith. She is published in three anthologies and blogs weekly at batteredhope.blogspot.com. On her weekly radio show, *Never Ever Give Up Hope,* she interviews people who have overcome tremendous odds and become victorious. She travels extensively as a motivational speaker for Christian women's groups and churches. She and her husband rescue dogs from abusive situations and give them a loving home.

Lydia E. Harris has been married to her college sweetheart, Milt, for forty-eight years. They have two married children and five grandchildren ranging from preschool to high school. Lydia earned a Master of Arts degree in home economics. She has written numerous articles, book reviews, devotionals, and stories. Focus on the Family's *Clubhouse* magazine for children publishes her recipes, which she develops and tests with her grandchildren. She writes the column, "A Cup of Tea with Lydia," and is called Grandma Tea by her grandchildren. Lydia has contributed to numerous books and is author of *Preparing My Heart for Grandparenting: For Grandparents at Any Stage of the Journey* (AMG Publishers).

Joyce Heiser is living her retirement dream as a published author. Her call to write came at age 57 in 2002. She has cofounded and led writer's groups in Wisconsin and South Dakota. Her award-winning devotions and personal essays are widely published in magazines and newsletters, online, and in several Amazon bestselling anthologies. She also sits on the board of South Dakota Authors Association. Her website is JoyceHeiser.com.

Karen R. Hessen's many writings have been published in six volumes of *Chicken Soup for the Soul, Guideposts, When God Makes Lemonade, RAIN Magazine 2013* and *2014, Vista, The Secret Place, The Mother's Heart Magazine, Help! I'm A Parent, God Makes Lemonade, CAP Connection, Apple Hill Cider Press, SSEEDS OF...Volume II: Anthology of Pacific Northwest Authors* and others. She writes the monthly columns, "Zap, Kackle, Plop" and "Out of the Ark" for *The Lincoln City News Guard*. Her latest work is included in the recent release of *Jesus Encounters.*

Victoria Hicks is a wife, mother and grandmother. She lives in Louisville, Kentucky with her husband, Gary. She enjoys being with their grandsons, reading, needlework, and researching ancestors. She has written articles and poetry for her church newsletter, "The Carillon," along with advent and Easter collections. She has written dialogue and co-written lyrics for both youth and adult choir productions, and enjoys writing fiction. She is a graduate of both courses at Institute of Children's Literature, and a member of Louisville Christian Writers. Active in her church, Victoria teaches the Shepherd Bible study class, is involved in choir, and is a member of Women's Missionary Union.

Larry C. Hoover told his story, "The Light" to his wife, Helen, who wrote it for him. They are retired, live in Northwest Arkansas, and volunteer at a Christian college. Larry helps in the maintenance department. Helen does data entry for the admissions office. Helen's devotions and personal stories are published in books and Christian hand-out papers.

Geneva Cobb Iijima writes for adults and children. She has 100 stories, articles and devotions published, including articles with Focus on the Family, *Decision Magazine* and *Guideposts*. She has published four books: *Object Lessons in Origami* (Standard) for use in teaching children; *The First Christmas in Origami* (Thomas Nelson), a family activity/devotion book; *The Way We Do It In Japan* (Albert Whitman), a children's picture book; and *Jesus Loves Us All* (Seed Faith Books), a children's picture book published in English, Japanese, Spanish and the five Quechua languages. Visit her at www.genevacobbiijima.com.

Sondra Kraak is a native of the Pacific Northwest. She thrives on the outdoors, music, quirky words, and a good book. She holds a B.A. in English and an M.A. in Biblical Studies. Her passions include blogging about spiritual truths, leading Bible studies, hiking with her family, serving as the accompanist at her church, and yanking up weeds from her North Carolina yard. She is a member of ACFW, a 2015 double semi-finalist in the Genesis contest, and winner of the 2015 Blue Ridge Mountains Christian Writers Conference unpublished novel contest (women's fiction).

Barbara Latta is a free-lance writer whose passion is to share how the grace of God can free us from the rules of religious tradition. Her articles, devotions, and poems have been published in several newspapers, magazines, and websites. She writes a monthly column for the *Pike Journal-Reporter* in Zebulon, Georgia. She is a board member of the East Metro Atlanta Christian Writers. She enjoys riding motorcycles with her Harley husband, and their biker travels are the inspiration for her blog, *Navigating Life's Curves*, visit her at barbaralatta.blogspot.com.

Yvonne Lehman is the author of 55 novels. She founded, and directed for 25 years, the Blue Ridge Mountains Christian Writers Conference and now directs the Blue Ridge Novelist Retreat held annually in October at Ridgecrest Conference Center, North Carolina. She lives in panoramic Black Mountain, North Carolina with her beautiful furry blond and white Pomeranian, Rigel, named after a Titanic survivor. Her latest books are *The Reluctant Schoolmarm* in *Reluctant Brides* collection (Barbour) and *Name that Tune* in *A Gentleman's Kiss (Barbour)*. Her non-fiction compilations are *Divine Moments, Christmas Moments, Spoken Moments,* and *Preciosus, Precocious Moments* (Grace). Her

50th book is *Hearts that Survive – A Novel of the Titanic* (Abingdon Press). She blogs with ChristiansRead and Novel Rocket.

Diana Leagh Matthews is a vocalist, speaker, writer, life coach, and genealogist. She is a 2011 graduate of Christian Communicators Conference and 2012 graduate of Christian Devotions Boot Camp. She has been published in several anthologies, including *My Love to You Always*, *I Believe in Heaven* and *Breaking the Chains*. She currently resides in upstate South Carolina. Visit her at DianaLeaghMatthews.com and alookthrutime.com.

Dianne Neal Matthews is the author of four daily devotional books including *The One Year Women of the Bible* (Tyndale House) and *Designed for Devotion: A 365-Day Journey from Genesis to Revelation* (Baker Books), which won a 2013 Selah Award. She also writes regularly for blogs and websites (such as CBN and More to Life), contributes to compilations (including Guideposts' *Mornings with Jesus*), and enjoys teaching at writers' conferences. Dianne is a CLASS graduate and a member of Christian Authors Network, American Christian Fiction Writers, and Toastmasters International. She and her husband, Richard, currently live in southeast Texas (which is nice but too far away from their children and three grandchildren). To learn more, please visit DianneNealMatthews.com.

Edie Melson is the author of numerous books, including *While My Soldier Serves,* a book of prayers for those with a loved one in the military (Worthy Inspired). As a sought-after speaker, she's encouraged and challenged audiences across the U.S. Connect with her on her website, EdieMelson.com and through social media.

Andrea Merrell is an author, editor, workshop leader, and writing mentor with a passion to encourage other writers, helping them sharpen their skills. She is Associate Editor for Christian Devotions Ministries and Lighthouse Publishing of the Carolinas. Andrea has been published online and in numerous anthologies. Her first book, *Murder of a Manuscript: Writing and Editing Tips to Keep Your Book Out of the Editorial Graveyard*, is available online through Amazon and Barnes and Noble. Her next book is *Praying for the Prodigal*. For more information or to contact her, visit andreamerrell.com or hewriteediting.com.

Marybeth Mitcham holds a B.S. in Biology, is completing her MPH in nutrition, and currently works as a tutor for Liberty University's Online

Writing Center. She is an emerging freelance author, whose writings have been published online. She recently was a guest on the Chris Fabry Live radio show, discussing her article *My Magnum Opus*, and is a public speaker for the pro-life movement. She is currently working on her first book. Marybeth lives with her family in the southern Adirondack region of New York.

Vicki H. Moss is Contributing Editor for *Southern Writers Magazine* and past Editor-at-Large. A columnist for the *American Daily Herald*, she's also a poet, author of *How to Write for Kids' Magazines* and *Writing with Voice*, a Precept Ministries leader and a Christian Communicators graduate. She has written for *Hopscotch* and *Boy's Quest* magazines for the last decade in addition to being published in *Christmas Moments*, *Divine Moments* and *Precious, Precocious Moments*, *SouthWest Sage, Country Woman, In the City, Borderlines*, Scotland's *Thistle Blower*, and *I Believe in Heaven*. She was selected to be a presenter of her fiction and creative nonfiction short stories for three conferences in a row at the Southern Women Writers Conference held at Rome, Georgia's Berry College. Vicki is also a speaker and on faculty for writers conferences. For more information visit livingwaterfiction.com.

Dee Dee Parker infuses wisps of Southern grace throughout both her writing and speaking. She is the author of a children's book, *Josie Jo's Got to Know*, written to benefit breast cancer research. She has contributed to numerous anthologies, such as *Chicken Soup for the Soul, Clothes Lines*, and *Christmas Presence*. Dee Dee writes for *ChristianDevotions.us, Guidepost* books, *Guidepost.or*g as well as Focus on the Family's *Clubhouse Jr.* magazine. Her first Christmas novella has landed in the hands of her agent and she eagerly anticipates its publication in the near future. Dee Dee lives snuggled among the North Carolina Appalachian Mountains with her husband Jim, a retired minister, and their spoiled Schnoodle, Greta. Email Dee Dee at deedeeparker@charter.net.

Linda Landreth Phelps has been a published poet since first grade, when "Little Teddy" was included in her church's newsletter. Professionally speaking, not much happened between that day and when she sold her first story to an international magazine forty-plus years later. She is currently the senior staff writer for a Williamsburg, Virginia regional publication and contributes on a regular basis to two others. Linda is at work on her first book, a World War II historical memoir based on her parents' wartime correspondence. Linda and her husband, Art, recently celebrated their forty-seventh anniversary and are enjoying an active retirement of travel and Christian ministry. They have two grown children and two grandsons.

Deborah M. Presnell, co-founder of Shine! Ministries**,** has been a speaker for women's events and teachers' organizations for twenty years. She is also a partner with the Polished Conference, an event for teen girls. She writes an inspirational blog, *Living Life Together,* and teaches Bible studies. Her speaking schedule includes teen conferences, women's church groups, MOPS', state conferences, and universities. She is author of *Shine! Radiating the Love of God.* Debbie became a Christian at the age of nine and is a member of Biltmore Baptist Church in Asheville, North Carolina. Visit her on her website: debbiepresnell.com

Kimberly Rae is an award-winning author of twenty books. She has been published over three hundred times and has work in five languages. Her romantic suspense novels on international human trafficking and missions — *Stolen Woman, Stolen Child,* and *Stolen Future* — are all Amazon bestsellers. Rae has lived in Bangladesh, Uganda, Kosovo, and Indonesia, but now writes from her home at the base of the Blue Ridge Mountains where she lives with her husband and two young children. Learn more at kimberlyrae.com.

Susan Holt Simpson is a freelance writer living in northern Kentucky. She has been married to her childhood sweetheart for twenty-seven years, and they are enjoying the adventures of life with three mostly-grown sons. As a literacy coach and a mothering mentor, Susan's volunteer work in the local community keeps her busy. She has written for Focus on the Family and writes online about parenting, gardening, and photography. Visit her at Sweet-Annabelle.blogspot.com or find her on various social media including Facebook, Instagram, Twitter and Pinterest.

Cindy Sproles is cofounder of Christian Devotions Ministries. She serves as the Executive Editor of ChristianDevotions.us and is the Devotional Acquisitions Editor for Lighthouse Publishing of the Carolinas. Cindy is a conference teacher, speaker, and mentor. Cindy' devotions are published in Christian newspapers across the eastern seaboard. She's the author of two non-fiction books and *Mercy's Rain*, an Appalachian Novel (Kregel Publications). Visit her at cindysproles.com.

Nate Stevens is a "missionary kid" who grew up in a Christian home and church. He has enjoyed a 30-year banking career in a variety of leadership roles.

He writes online devotions for Christian Devotions Ministries, devotions for his home church (Calvary Church in Charlotte, North Carolina), and articles for several publications. His book *Matched 4 Marriage – Meant 4 Life* is available at all major book retailers. His next book, *Deck Time in the Storm*, is currently in production. He speaks at conferences, seminars and Bible study groups for singles, young adults, young marrieds, and youth. He lives near Charlotte, North Carolina and is an active dad with his two awesome kids, Melissa and Mitchell. Contact and book information may be found at: www.natestevens.net.

Annmarie B. Tait resides in Conshohocken, Pennsylvania with her husband, Joe Beck. In addition to writing stories about her large Irish Catholic family and the memories they made, she also enjoys singing and recording Irish and American folk songs with her husband. Among her other passions are cooking, sewing and crocheting. Annmarie has over fifty stories published in various anthologies including *Chicken Soup for the Soul* and the *Patchwork Path* series. You may contact her at irishbloom@aol.com.

Ann Tatlock is a three-time winner of the major Christy Award. She has also won the Midwest Independent Publishers Association "Book of the Year" in fiction for *All the Way Home* and *I'll Watch the Moon*. Publishers Weekly calls her "one of Christian fiction's better wordsmiths." Ann lives with her husband and daughter in Asheville, North Carolina.

Joni Vance is an award-winning author of non-fiction and is currently writing a murder mystery. She has participated in various state and national writers groups. After realizing her dream of moving to the Asheville area, she is honored to be a member of the Black Mountain/Blue Ridge Writers group. A senior technical writer with a major software corporation, Joni develops online user help files and reference manuals. Having a Master's degree in Education, she has taught children and adults, as well as developing curriculum, course materials, and user manuals in the areas of education, telecommunications, and healthcare.

Dr. Rhett H. Wilson, Sr. pastors The Spring Church in Laurens, South Carolina. He enjoys life with his wife Tracey and their three children, Hendrix, Anna-Frances, and Dawson. The Wilsons explore waterfalls in the Carolinas, tube down mountain streams, and look forward to March Madness basketball each year. Rhett likes reading legal thrillers and Southern fiction, writing, and listening to country, classical, and Broadway music. Rhett and

Tracey have released two CDs, *Lead Me On* and *Offered Praises*. He is writing a book titled *Seven Words to Pray for My Family*. Rhett is available to speak or sing at your church. Visit his blog, *Faith, Family, and Friends,* at rhettwilson.blogspot.com.

Simon Wilson is the sixteen-year-old son of Steve and Cindy Wilson, both of whom have contributed to *Moments* books. He wrote his story when he was fourteen, after the deaths of his grandfathers. Simon is home-schooled and is an avid athlete, having trained for the past nine years to be a tennis player.

Ann Greenleaf Wirtz is the author of *The Henderson County Curb Market: A Blue Ridge Heritage Since 1924* and *Sorrow Answered: A Journey of Grace*. She was published in *A Chicken Soup for the Soul Christmas*, 2007. She formerly wrote the weekly "Crossroads" for the *Times-News*, which still publishes her work. Each December a nostalgic remembrance appears in *The Pulse*. Ann is the mother of one dear son and daughter-in-law and has two precious grandchildren. She resides in the Blue Ridge Mountains of Hendersonville, North Carolina, with her loving husband, Patrick.

www.ingramcontent.com/pod-product-compliance
Lightning Source LLC
Chambersburg PA
CBHW070455100426
42743CB00010B/1629